THE COMPLETE WORKS OF
CHRISTOPHER MARLOWE

Despite the modern fascination with Marlowe, and in particular with his *Dr Faustus*, there has been no edition of his works which not only gives them in the original spelling—with full textual apparatus—but also supplies a detailed commentary. The Oxford English texts *Complete Works of Christopher Marlowe*, edited in three volumes by Roma Gill, supplies the need for a fully annotated scholarly treatment of the works.

The present volume is devoted to *Dr Faustus*, which is now edited from the edition of 1604. A new theory of this text and its transmission is presented in an introductory essay, '*Dr Faustus*, the textual problem'; the play is critically discussed in another essay, '*Dr Faustus*, the real problem'. Differing theories of the text are outlined in an appendix, and another appendix selects the substantial passages which make the 1616 edition of the play unlike the 1604 version. Extracts from *The English Faustbook*, the main source of Marlowe's play, are also appended.

ROMA GILL is a freelance writer and lecturer; her previous editions include *The Plays of Christopher Marlowe* (Oxford, 1971) and ten texts in the Oxford School Shakespeare Series. She was formerly a General Editor of the New Mermaid Texts (for which she edited three plays), and Reader in English Literature at the University of Sheffield.

THE COMPLETE WORKS
OF
CHRISTOPHER
MARLOWE

EDITED BY
ROMA GILL

VOLUME II
Dr Faustus

CLARENDON PRESS · OXFORD

1990

Oxford University Press, Walton Street, Oxford OX2 6DP

Oxford New York Toronto
Delhi Bombay Calcutta Madras Karachi
Petaling Jaya Singapore Hong Kong Tokyo
Nairobi Dar es Salaam Cape Town
Melbourne Auckland

and associated companies in
Berlin Ibadan

Oxford is a trade mark of Oxford University Press

Published in the United States
by Oxford University Press, New York

British Library Cataloguing in Publication Data
Marlowe, Christopher, 1564–1593
The complete works of Christopher Marlowe.
(Oxford English texts)
Vol. 2, Dr Faustus
I. Title   II. Gill, Roma
822′.3
ISBN 0–19–812769–3

Library of Congress Cataloging in Publication Data
Marlowe, Christopher, 1564–1593.
Dr. Faustus
p.   cm.—(The complete works of Christopher Marlowe; v. 2)
Bibliography: p.
1. Faust, d. ca. 1540—Drama.   I. Title.   II. Title: Doctor
Faustus.   III. Series: Marlowe, Christopher, 1564–1593.   Works.
1987; v. 2.   PR2661.G5   1987 vol. 2
[PR2664.A2]   822′.3—dc20
89–9354
ISBN 0–19–812769–3

Typeset by Eta Services (Typesetters) Ltd., Beccles, Suffolk
Printed and bound in
Great Britain by Biddles Ltd.
Guildford and Kings Lynn

In Memory of my Mother

ACKNOWLEDGEMENTS

My work on *Dr Faustus* started in 1964, at the instigation of Professor Philip Brockbank, then General Editor of Benn's New Mermaid Series of dramatic texts. I owe thanks to him as the first, but by no means only, begetter of my interest in Marlowe. I must also thank Janet Bartlam and Mark Burnett, who have assisted with the final stages of the preparation of this manuscript, and Jan Greenough who read the proofs. I am grateful for the help and encouragement of a generous grant from the British Academy.

To itemize the assistance, and nominate the helpers, for the years between 1964 and 1987 would be labour lost; once again, 'my thanks to all at once, and to each one.'

R.G.

CONTENTS

Illustrations

PREFACE

THE present text is based on the earliest extant edition of *Dr Faustus* (the A text) which was published in 1604 and which I believe to be founded on the manuscript used as a prompt-book by the Admiral's Men for their earliest performances. In general the play is well printed and needs little editorial interference. Two comic episodes (here identified as scenes 6 and 8) were initially printed together; they were first separated in the 1616 edition and set in their present positions. Scene divisions throughout the play are indicated in square brackets, and the uses of *i* and *j*, *u* and *v* have been normalized. In speech prefixes the names of the characters (usually abbreviated) have been silently expanded and standardized to conform to the list of *Dramatis Personae* supplied here. For the name of Faustus's familiar spirit the spelling MEPHASTOPHILIS has been adopted for editorial usage, since this is the form most often found in the A text. For the most part (and unless otherwise noted), stage directions have been left in their original forms and locations which, I believe, demonstrate the prompt-book basis of the 1604 text.

Proper names are uniformly italicized, although the 1604 edition's usage is somewhat haphazard; departures from the copy-text's practice are listed, with other accidental emendations, at the end of the play. Substantive variants, with their sources, are recorded in the *apparatus criticus*. Major variants in the 1616 edition are printed in Appendix B, and the relationship between the 1604 and 1616 editions is discussed in Appendix C. The first Appendix supplies the outline of the Faust story as Marlowe found it in his source narrative, *The English Faustbook*; occasional minor similarities between the play and its source are mentioned in the Commentary, as are rejected minor variants from the 1616 and other editions of the play.

Title-pages of the two early editions are reproduced.

Date and source

My analysis of the text will show the impossibility of assigning a date to *Dr Faustus*; the Horse-courser's allusion to 'Dr Lopus' (scene 10 line 37) was probably introduced after the execution of Lopez in February 1594, but Marlowe's own share cannot be later than 30 May 1593—the date of his murder. The date of Marlowe's source suggests that the play must have been written towards the end of the dramatist's life. Accounts of the famous German magician were collected and published in Frankfurt in 1587, but Marlowe's play bears some close resemblances to an English translation, *The English Faustbook* (see Appendix A) whose earliest extant edition is dated 1592.

References and Abbreviations

1. Early texts of Dr Faustus*:*

A1	*The Tragicall History of D. Faustus* (London, 1604; reprinted 1609 (A2), and 1611 (A3))
B1	*The Tragicall History of the Life and Death of Doctor Faustus* (London, 1616; reprinted 1619 (B2), 1620 (B3), 1624 (B4), 1628 (B5), and 1631 (B6))

2. Major editions of Dr Faustus, *cited by the name of the editor:*

Boas	*The Tragicall History of Doctor Faustus*, ed. F. S. Boas (London, 1932).
Bowers	*The Complete Works of Christopher Marlowe*, ed. Fredson Bowers (Cambridge, 1974).
Bullen	*The Works of Christopher Marlowe*, ed. A. H. Bullen (London, 1885).
Dyce	*The Works of Christopher Marlowe*, ed. A. Dyce (London, 1850).
Greg	*Marlowe's 'Dr Faustus' 1604–1616: Parallel Texts*, ed. W. W. Greg (Oxford, 1950).
Jump	*Doctor Faustus*, ed. John Jump (London, 1962).
Ormerod & Wortham	*Dr Faustus: the A Text*, ed. David Ormerod and Christopher Wortham (Nedlands, Western Australia, 1985).

Tucker Brooke   *The Works of Christopher Marlowe*, ed. C. F. Tucker Brooke (Oxford, 1910).

Quotations from Marlowe's other works are taken from *The Complete Works of Christopher Marlowe*, volume I: Translations, ed. Roma Gill (Oxford, 1987), and from *The Complete Works of Christopher Marlowe*, ed. Fredson Bowers (Cambridge, 1974).

3. Quotations from the works of authors frequently cited throughout the volume are taken from the following editions:

Henslowe   *Henslowe's Diary*, ed. R. A. Foakes and R. T. Rickert (Cambridge, 1961).

Nashe   *The Works of Thomas Nashe*, ed. R. B. McKerrow (Oxford, 1904), with corrections and supplementary notes by F. P. Wilson (Oxford, 1958; reprinted 1966); referred to in the text as McKerrow.

Ovid   *Ovid's Metamorphoses*, trans. Arthur Golding (1567), ed. John Frederick Nims (New York, 1965).

Shakespeare   The Riverside Edition, ed. G. Blakemore Evans *et al.* (Boston, 1974).

See the Select Bibliography for full references to these and other relevant works.

4. Other abbreviations:

EFB   *The English Faustbook*, 1592 (parts reprinted in Appendix A).

Om.   Omitted.

SD   Stage direction.

SR   Stationers' Register.

Tilley   *A Dictionary of the Proverbs in England in the Sixteenth and Seventeenth Centuries*, compiled by M. P. Tilley (Ann Arbor, 1950).

INTRODUCTION

Dr Faustus: The Textual Problem

Dr Faustus has remarkably few problems for an editor—once the surviving facts have been honestly faced.

The play was not performed until after Marlowe's death in 1593. In the months following the assassination—perhaps taking advantage of the publicity—there were more performances than usual of *Tamburlaine*, *The Jew of Malta*, and *The Massacre at Paris*; but it was not until September 1594 that *Dr Faustus* entered the repertoire of The Lord Admiral's Men, when their financier, Philip Henslowe, recorded the takings in his *Diary*: '30 of september 1594 Rd at docter ffostose ... iij^{li} xij^s' (p. 24). Although the play was not designated 'ne', which seems to have been the impresario's way of indicating a new work, the large sum taken at this performance suggests that the play was in fact new to the stage: no performance of any other play (even the 'ne' ones) returned so much money that year (Henslowe, p. 25). Further entries in the *Diary* speak of the play's continued success; and then in 1602 Henslowe makes a different kind of note:

Lent unto the companye the 22 of novembr 1602
to paye unto w^m Bvrde & Samwell Rowle   iiij^{li}
for ther adicyones in docter fostes the some of ... (p. 206)

The sum was large—testimony at once to the play's popularity (Henslowe would not have invested so much money in a loser), and to the size of the additions made to the play by Birde and Rowley.

Any number of reasons might have contributed to a decision to 'modernize' *Dr Faustus*: although a popular play, it must have seemed 'old-fashioned' and 'Elizabethan' to the more sophisticated, Jacobean audience in the seventeenth century; and the actor Edward Alleyn (Henslowe's son-in-law, and his theatrical business-partner) was about to leave the company for which he had played leading roles such as Barabas in *The Jew of Malta* and the eponymous hero of *Tamburlaine*. But whatever the reason for the 'adicyones', it seems that the company must have had a new prompt-book, so that they could be persuaded to part with their old play and surrender it to the publishers.

Dr Faustus was entered in the Stationers' Register on 7 January 1601:

Tho. Busshell Entred for his copye under the handes. of m^r Doctor
     Barlowe, and the Wardens. A booke called the plaie of
     Doctor Faustus.

Whether any printing followed this registration, and how soon after the formal entry, it is impossible to say: of the first three known editions of the play there exist, altogether, only five copies, so it would not be surprising to find that an entire first edition had been lost. The earliest surviving edition (which exists in a unique copy) was published in 1604:

THE | TRAGICALL | History of D. Faustus. | *As it hath bene Acted by the Right | Honorable the Earle of Nottingham his servants.* Written by Ch. Marl. | [device] | LONDON | Printed by V.S. for Thomas Bushell. 1604.
STC 17429; Bodleian Library, Oxford: Malone 233 (3)

For general convenience, this is referred to as the A text. Subsequent editions, with some minor corrections, were published in 1609 (A2), and 1611 (A3); there are three extant copies of the former (Huntington Library, California; Petworth House, Sussex; and the State Library in Hamburg), and only one (Huntington Library) of the 1611 edition.

In 1616 a very different text was published; this (for convenience referred to as the B text) also survives in a unique copy:

The Tragicall History | of the Life and Death | of *Doctor Faustus.* | Written by *Ch. Mar.* | [woodcut] | LONDON, | Printed for *Iohn Wright,* and are to be sold at his shop | without Newgate, at the signe of the | Bible. 1616.
STC 17432; British Library, C.34.d.26

This version was reprinted five times before 1633; the title-page of the second (1619) edition bears information that could well have been given three years earlier, in the claim that it is 'With new Additions'. The B text contains a variety of episodes which are not found in A—episodes such as those involving the claims of the rival pope, Bruno, and the discomfiture of the insulting knights at the imperial court. Other clownage scenes have been tidied up—

the crude foolery of the clown who encountered the devils is now more polite; but the trickery with the vintner's goblet is also modified (perhaps the jugglers were no longer available). And much of the responsibility for the damnation of Faustus has been switched from the protagonist himself to the diabolic powers.

But the 'new Additions' are not the only features that distinguish the B text from its predecessors in the tradition of the A text; there are also significant deletions. Some of these suggest that a man of straightforward common sense has been at work on the copy supplied to him. When, for instance, this 'editor' could not understand the word that appears as 'scaenes' in scene 1 line 51, he omitted it and printed instead simply 'Lines, Circles, Letters, Characters'; and recognizing that the present tense was no longer appropriate, he altered the line about the plate fleet 'That yearly stuffes old *Philips* treasury' (line 132) to read 'stuff'd'. More important, however, were the cuts made in dutiful obedience to an act of Parliament that became law in 1606, the 'Act of Abuses':

An Acte to restraine Abuses of Players

... That if at any tyme or tymes ... any person or persons doe or shall in any Stage play ... jestingly or prophanely speake or use the holy Name of God or of Christ Jesus, or of the Holy Ghoste or of the Trinitie, which are not to be spoken but with feare and reverence, shall forfeite for everie such Offence by hym or them committed Tenne Pounde.

Threatened by such a penalty, the Faustus of the B text does not try to 'leape up to [his] God'; instead he makes a feeble attempt to 'leape up to heaven'; Christ's blood no longer 'streames in the firmament', and the threatening arm and angry brow do not belong to anyone.

For the most part the edited and censored B text is of historical interest rather than practical use in preparing a modern edition of *Dr Faustus*. The A text, on which the present edition is based, provides more than adequate material for the recovery of the play that was performed in 1594, sixteen months after Marlowe was murdered. These are, I admit, very personal opinions (the opposing views are described in Appendix C); and Greg's challenge must still be answered: 'anyone who maintains that the A Text preserves substantially the original version of the play will have to do a lot of explaining' (*Parallel Texts*, p. 21).

The comic scenes are the ones that have to be explained; no one has ever doubted that the first and last soliloquies are in Marlowe's finest style, or that the Scholars' praise of Helen, as well as Faustus's own apostrophe to the vision, are uttered in the master's mighty lines. But the comedy of the play's central scenes is less clearly characterized, and much of the time it does not seem to speak Marlowe's own sense of humour as this is found in *Tamburlaine* and *The Jew of Malta*—or even *The Massacre at Paris*. In all these plays the humour is cool, witty, and purposeful: the cruelty of the play is underlined by the laughter as tension releases into near-hysteria (rather than relaxation) in *1 Tamburlaine*, when the conqueror mounts to his throne on the back of the subdued Bajazeth (IV. ii); or when the two Friars mourn the unravished virginity, more than the death, of Abigail in *The Jew of Malta* (III. vi). Indeed, the Prologue to *1 Tamburlaine* scorns the stage comedy popular at the time, dismissing 'such conceits as clownage keeps in pay'—but this is an apt description of the material used in *Dr Faustus* to span the four and twenty years between signing the infernal contract and its terminal date.

I suggest that when Marlowe died he left his play on Dr Faustus unfinished: it had a beginning and an ending (both inspired by *The English Faustbook* (*EFB*)), but not much more to fill the two hours' traffic of the stage. The play's central episodes are disappointing after the masterly first scenes—but so too are the same episodes in *EFB*, which easily degenerates into a jest-book with a few moralizing tracts. Marlowe might have abandoned his play because he was bored or frustrated by the banality of his source—and it fell to Henslowe (or some other) to find means of preparing the work for performance.

One writer whose name was associated with Marlowe's was Thomas Nashe: the two were near-contemporaries at Cambridge; Nashe's name appears (without justification) on the title-page of *Dido Queene of Carthage*; and Gabriel Harvey insulted Nashe as 'the son of a mule, a raw grammarian, a babbling sophister . . . a dodkin author whose gayest flourishes are Gascoigne's weeds, or Tarleton's tricks, or Greene's cranks or Marlowe's bravados' (*Pierce's Supererogation* (1593)). The relationship between the two is by no means simple, but their known association might have suggested the name of Nashe to whatever kind of literary executor it was who attempted to see *Dr Faustus* on to the stage. Certainly Nashe recommends himself for the character of Wagner as he appears in scenes 2 and 4: Nashe's phrases are frequent in Wagner's mouth as the featureless choric presenter expands, for a short time, into the mould of Miles, Friar Bacon's 'subsizar' in Greene's *Friar Bacon and Friar Bungay* (?1589). The relationships between Miles and Bacon, Wagner and Faustus are academic rather than feudal—pupil:teacher, not servant:master. Impoverished undergraduates, both Miles and Wagner are repaid for their domestic services with a smattering of education; they hold positions of confidence, and they show a cheerful pride in these, and in their scholastic attainment. Wagner's first appearance (scene 2) is almost a solo act, as he parades his Latin and his logic (in mimicry of Faustus) before the bewildered Scholars. In scene 4, although he intends to imitate his master by becoming himself a master, Wagner in fact plays 'straight man' to the Clown, who inaugurates a sequence of what for Italians (in the *commedia dell' arte*) are called *lazzi*,[1] and which Thomas Pettitt has called 'dramaturgical formulas' and compared to the verbal formulas which are the backbone of traditional narrative genres such as the ballad, the epic, and the romance.[2] Pettitt defines a 'dramaturgical formula' as 'A sequence of action, involving movement, gesture and (although not necessarily) speech, which occurs in recognizably cognate forms in a number of different plays.' In *Dr Faustus* he identifies several different types of formula: the low comedy sequence of the hiring of the Clown, and the stolen cup; formulas from the mumming plays (such as the masque of devils, and the 'shew' of the Deadly Sins); and those episodes which find their counterparts in the morality plays—the Good and Evil Counsellors, the dagger offered as a temptation to suicide; and the various processions and dumbshows.

The actor who played the Clown in *Dr Faustus* must also have had the Clown's role in the moralistic comedy *A Looking-Glass for London*, written by Thomas Lodge and Robert Greene, which was entered in the Stationers' Register in March 1593/4. In this play he is variously called 'Clown' and 'Adam'. Scene xv in *A Looking-Glass* shows Adam escorting his master's wife home from the inn. The devil appears, and offers to carry Adam—who has in him

[1] Cf. K. M. Lea, *Italian Popular Comedy* (Oxford, 1934).
[2] Thomas Pettitt, 'Formulaic Dramaturgy in *Dr Faustus*', in '*A Poet and a Filthy Playmaker: Essays on Christopher Marlowe*, edited by Kenneth Friedenreich, Roma Gill, and Constance Kuriyama (New York, 1988), p. 169.

some traces of the Morality Vice—away to hell. The Clown, his confidence strengthened by alcohol and incantation, stands his ground: '*Nominus patrus*, I blesse me from thee, and I coniure thee to tell me who thou art' (G3^r). Reaching for his 'cudgell', he attacks until the devil pleads that he is mortally wounded; Adam triumphs with the boast:

> Then may I count my selfe I think a tall man, that am able to kill a diuell. Now who dare deale with me in the parish, or what wench in *Ninivie* will not loue me, when they say, there goes he that beate the diuell. (G3^v)

These lines were introduced into the episode in *Dr Faustus* where the devils are invoked by Wagner for the hiring of the reluctant servant—the Clown. But the Clown here does not beat the devils; he only entertains the possibility:

> Ile knocke them, they were never so knockt since they were divels, say I should kill one of them, what would folkes say? do ye see yonder tall fellow in the round slop, hee has kild the divell, so I should be cald kill divell all the parish over.

Although in *Dr Faustus* the action of calling up the devil parodies the main plot, the Clown's lines do not arise naturally from the situation, as they do in *A Looking-Glass*; it seems likely, then, that *Dr Faustus* was the borrower.

But the lines from *A Looking-Glass for London* were not this Clown's only contribution to *Dr Faustus*. The actor-lists in E. K. Chambers's *Elizabethan Stage* (Oxford, 1923, ii. 296) identify an actor called John Adams (who presumably—as was the custom with comedians—gave his own name to his parts). He played with Sussex's Men in 1576, and with The Queen's Men in 1583 and 1588; and his reputation was good enough to link him with Richard Tarlton in the memory of the Stage-keeper in Jonson's *Bartholomew Fair* (1614), when he remembers how 'Adams, the rogue, ha' leaped and capered upon him [Tarlton] and ha' dealt his vermin about as though they had cost him nothing' (Induction to *Bartholomew Fair*, ll. 38–40; *The Works of Ben Jonson*, ed. C. H. Herford and Percy Simpson (Oxford, 1927)). Adams, one must deduce, was the kind of clown scathingly described by Hamlet in the Q1 advice to the players, who 'keepes one sute of jeasts, as a man is known by one sute of Apparell' (III. ii).

He produces this 'sute of jeasts' in response to Wagner's promise that he shall be provided with 'staves acre'—a common insect-repellent. After a nicely calculated delay comes the required (and expected) response: 'why then belike, if I were your man, I should be ful of vermine'. The routine proceeds through Wagner's threat to 'turne al the lice about thee into familiars, and they shal teare thee in peeces'. The Clown's contribution—through John Adams's personal gimmick with the fleas—brings the comedy routine into even closer contact with the main action, where the infernal powers are always ready to threaten the backsliding Faustus: 'If thou repent, devils will teare thee in peeces.'

Adams and Nashe (if indeed Nashe is responsible for the character—as distinct from the choric—Wagner) may have directed most of the comedy scenes, but they were probably not unwilling to accept offerings from other members of the cast. In the juggling episode between the Clowns and the Vintner (scene 8), Rafe is instructed to provide his own terms of abuse: 'I scorne you: and you are but a &c.' Interestingly, the licence has been revoked in the B text's version of this scene—a sign perhaps that the later text is preparing for the more sophisticated tastes of the seventeenth century, when the kind of patchworking that seems to have cobbled up the middle of the A text was despised. Letoy in Brome's *Antipodes* (1638) glances superciliously back to:

> the days of Tarlton & Kempe,
> Before the stage was purg'd from barbarisme,
> And brought to the perfection it now shines with.
> Then fooles & jesters spent their wits, because
> The Poets were wise enough to save ther owne.

Dr Faustus: The Real Problem[1]

Most of the additions in the B text are trivial—expansions of the
comic scenes in Rome, at the imperial court, and at the entertainment of the Duke of Vanholt. Only one, the related episodes
inserted into scene 13, significantly affects Marlowe's composition.
But—by a nice dramatic irony—concentration on this section
affords access to the original play, and suggests at least one interpretation of the dramatist's intention.

B's scene (Appendix B, scene 13) opens with the ascent of
Lucifer, Belzebub, and Mephostophilis, who announce their
arrival 'from infernall *Dis*' to take a voyeuristic pleasure in the
agony of Faustus's final hour. This calls for a more sophisticated
staging (perhaps a balcony) than A requires; and the presence of
the diabolic spectators must surely distract the audience's atten-
tion from the protagonist, distancing them from Faustus when he
speaks to the Scholars—although the disjointed prose here surely
calls for maximum audience sympathy.

After Faustus's confession to the Scholars, B's Good and Bad
Angels make their final appearances, respectively reproaching and
gloating. In the A text the Angels depart soon after the signing of
the infernal contract, staying only long enough to articulate the
doctrine of repentance; unusually, the Good Angel has the last
word (scene 5 lines 261–65):

FAUSTUS   Ist not too late?

             Enter GOOD ANGELL *and* EVILL.

EVIL ANGEL   Too late.
GOOD ANGEL   Never too late, if *Faustus* can repent.
EVIL ANGEL   If thou repent divels shall teare thee in peeces.
GOOD ANGEL   Repent, & they shal never race thy skin.

                                                   Exeunt.

They perform the same function, at the same point in the play, in
the B text; but the 'adicyones' allow for a further appearance in
scene 13—which again calls for a more elaborate staging for its

---

[1] The first draft of this paper was read to a conference of the Société Française Shakespeare at the Sorbonne, Paris, in December 1981 and published with the *Actes de Congrès* in
Théâtre et Idéologies: Marlowe, Shakespeare, ed. M. T. Jones-Davies (Paris, 1982).

melodrama. The stage direction (probably originating in a theatrical manuscript) demands '*Musicke while the Throne descends*', and the Good Angel points out to Faustus what he has lost:

> *Faustus* behold,
> In what resplendant glory thou hadst set
> In yonder throne, like those bright shining Saints,
> And triumpht over hell . . .

The last line of his speech prepares for the standard medieval image of hell: 'The jawes of hell are open to receive thee', and the Angel's exit is followed by the stage direction '*Hell is discovered*', where doubtless what was revealed was the familiar 'Hell mought' which apparently belonged to the Admiral's Men in 1598.[2] The Bad Angel proceeds to remark Pinteresque kitchen detail:

> There are the Furies tossing damned soules,
> On burning forkes: their bodies boyle in lead.
> There are live quarters broyling on the coles,
> That ne'er can die.

Such a 'popular' concept of hell—localized, and expressed in terms of physical torment—is not incompatible with the abstract state described by Mephastophilis early in the play when he asserts the omnipresence of hell:

> Why this is hel, nor am I out of it:
> Thinkst thou that I who saw the face of God,
> And tasted the eternal joyes of heaven,
> Am not tormented with ten thousand hels,
> In being depriv'd of everlasting blisse. (scene 3 lines 76–80)

The 'adicyones' so far discussed have only vulgarized, without actually damaging, *Dr Faustus*; but there are six lines in this B text expansion that cannot be included in the general justification of the passage on grounds of theatrical effectiveness and ideological insignificance; after his confession to the Scholars, Dr Faustus confronts his familiar, and attempts to shift the blame for his predicament (scene 13 lines 90–1):

> O thou bewitching fiend, 'twas thy temptation,
> Hath rob'd me of eternall happinesse.

---

[2] Henslowe, p. 206.

The 'bewitching fiend' is triumphant, and relieves Faustus of all responsibility:

> I doe confesse it *Faustus*, and rejoyce;
> 'Twas I, that when thou wer't i'the way to heaven,
> Damb'd up thy passage, when thou took'st the booke,
> To view the Scriptures, then I turn'd the leaves
> And led thine eye.

Philip Brockbank, accepting B's additional material as part of Marlowe's original intention, reacted to these lines as 'A terrifying speech, recoiling upon our whole experience of the play'.[3] In 1965 it seemed to me that 'The whole nature of the play is changed by this addition';[4] and I still think that these few lines, which I now see to be without any bibliographical authority, are enough to change a magnificent tragedy into a cynical morality play, reducing its unique, intelligent, and responsible protagonist to a mere puppet, and subverting the essentially Christian ideology of a play whose author was popularly (and paradoxically) supposed to be 'Not inferior to any . . . in Atheisme and impietie'.[5]

The first soliloquy both tolerates and demands frequent examination. The opening of the play is comparable with that of *The Jew of Malta*: there is an expository speech by a 'Chorus' figure—who is Machiavelli in *The Jew*, and the doctor/expositor of the morality plays in *Dr Faustus*. The plays' protagonists are 'discovered', engaged in a characteristic activity: Barabas counts his shekels, and Faustus reviews his library. The soliloquy is some sixty lines long, but it represents the thought-processes of years. Faustus does not act on the spur of the moment: he has spent a lifetime (almost) mastering and evaluating the different subjects, turning to medicine when logic failed to satisfy, and to law when the physician's art disappointed him.

In this opening speech Marlowe establishes Faustus as a man of learning and experience, whose name does not sound incongruous in the impressive roll-call of Galen, Justinian, and Jerome, with whom he shares a *lingua franca*. The Latin quotations form, of course, the chief means whereby Faustus's authority is established. The fact that they are not always accurate is unimportant:

[3] J. P. Brockbank, *Marlowe: 'Dr Faustus'* (1962), p. 55.

[4] *Dr Faustus*, ed. Roma Gill (1965), p. xviii.

[5] Thomas Beard, *The Theatre of God's Judgements* (1597), p. 149.

this is a play, not a doctoral dissertation; and only a modern editor (or student with an annotated edition) is likely to observe that '*Aristotles* workes' did not provide the formulation '*Bene disserere est finis logices.*' Theatre audiences would be more likely to respect the Latin than question the attribution.

A more critical reaction, however, seems to be expected from the audience when, having dismissed the whole of the Cambridge secular curriculum, Faustus turns to theology: 'When all is done, Divinitie is best.' He claims to quote from '*Jeromes* Bible': '*Si peccasse negamus, fallimur, & nulla est in nobis veritas*'; and, as usual, the Latin is followed by an English version:

> If we say that we have no sinne,
> We deceive our selves, and theres no truth in us. (scene 1 lines 42–3)

The Latin, however, is not that of the Vulgate; Marlowe is ascribing to '*Jeromes* Bible' his own translation of a remembered sentence, which originates in the First Epistle General of John (1: 8). Here it is possible to remark a dramatic irony, readily appreciated by those whose memories can supply the next verse from the Epistle—which would have solved the doctor's dilemma:

> If we confess our sins, he is faithful and just to forgive us our sins, and to cleanse us from all unrighteousness.

But Faustus's English quotation does not, in fact, come immediately from the Bible; the words he uses (quoting accurately) are those of the 1559 Book of Common Prayer where they are separated from the consolation of the Epistle's verse 9, being used to preface the exhortation to repentance which, with the Order for General Confession, directly follows. If the Book of Common Prayer is recognized as the immediate source for this sentence, there is the risk of some diminution in the dramatic irony, since this depends on the context supplied by the Bible. On the other hand, it redeems Faustus from the charge of impetuousness in this serious matter, and inaccuracy in a vital quotation.

The Prayer Book sentence forms the minor premise in a syllogism whose major premise has already been stated with incredulous horror (evidenced in the exclamation and repetition):

> *Stipendium peccati mors est*: ha, *Stipendium, &c.*
> The reward of sinne is death: thats hard. (lines 39–40)

Formulated in these terms, the syllogism is capable of only one
solution; and the scholar 'that was wont to make [Wittenberg]
schooles ring with, *sic probo*' (scene 2 lines 1–2) demonstrates his
mastery of logic:

> Why then belike we must sinne,
> And so consequently die. (lines 44–5)

The whole soliloquy has been driving towards this moment when
Faustus experiences the ultimate frustration of all earthly ambition. It is comparable to the last scene of *2 Tamburlaine* where the
shepherd-warrior, having called for a map, proudly demonstrates
the extent of his conquests—all the time interspersing his boasts
with the despairing lament 'And shall I die, and this unconquered'
(V. iii. 150). Tamburlaine's frustration is final, but Faustus,
having decided that he 'must die an everlasting death', seeks to
evade his predicament by turning to magic, hoping—through the
acquisition of new skills—to achieve a 'dominion [which] | Stret-
cheth as farre as doth the minde of man' (line 61).

There is a terrible irony here. Faustus has just demonstrated—
superbly—the power of the human mind, which can wrestle with
the complexities of logic and law, and understand the workings of
the human body. And at the same time he has demonstrated the
limitations of man's understanding.

The soliloquy also asserts the *individuality* of Marlowe's
protagonist. This is no 'Everyman' figure, the prototype of
humanum genus who is the hero common to all the medieval morality plays. Dr Faustus is given not only a local habitation and a
name, but also parents ('base of stocke'), and a *curriculum vitae*
which even includes publications (the 'billes hung up as monuments'). Most important of all for an understanding of his unique
personality is the exhibition provided in the soliloquy of an in-
dependent mind, actively engaged in an effort to understand some
of the fundamental problems of human existence. Dr Faustus is
like Shakespeare's tragic heroes in his attempts to question the
universe; and, like them, he 'is himself alone' (*Coriolanus*, I. iv.
51).

The conjuration scene does nothing to destroy this impression
of Faustus as a man of powerful intellect and personal charisma.
He has acquired a new skill, and he delights in its use (although
those familiar with techniques of diabolical invocation might note

a characteristic carelessness when Faustus forgets to specify the form that the spirit should assume—an omission that Marlowe uses to good theatrical effect: the stage direction that follows the conjuration (scene 3) is simply (in both texts) *Enter a Divell*, but B's copy—which, I suggest, was also a prompt-book—supplied the English word 'Dragon' in the middle of the Latin formula. This I interpret as an anticipatory direction, warning the book-keeper to be ready with the appropriate monster: the properties of the Admiral's Men included 'j dragon in fostes',[6] and the title-page of the B quarto depicts Faustus standing within his circle, book in hand, contemplating a creature with wings and tail that seems to have risen through the floor.[7]

Marlowe shows remarkable skill in manipulating the mood of this scene from the melodrama of the opening, where Faustus must first conjure up the impression of darkness and night which

> Leapes from th'antartike world unto the skie,
> And dimmes the welkin with her pitchy breath. (scene 3 lines 3–4)

This prepares for the invocation of the devil (which even today is awesome in its Latin sonority) and the appearance of the devil-dragon; then the horror is dispelled with a joke—and Faustus incidentally affirms his Protestant sympathies as he instructs the apparition to:

> Goe and returne an old Franciscan Frier,
> That holy shape becomes a divell best. (lines 25–6)

Between the disappearance of the 'Dragon' and the entrance of Mephastophilis the audience has time to calm down, while a slightly hysterical Faustus congratulates himself on the efficacy of his conjuring.

The first discussion with Mephastophilis is—or should be—a very sobering experience. The unhappy devil speaks with a bleak infinity of misery and experience to the uncomprehending doctor who is exuberant, over-confident, and so ignorant that he can offer to instruct his mentor;

> Learne thou of *Faustus* manly fortitude,
> And scorne those joyes thou never shalt possesse. (lines 85–6)

---

[6] Henslowe, p. 320.
[7] See illustration, p. 107; the subject is also discussed in the Commentary p. 65.

The perfect description of his conduct here is in Isabella's words to Angelo when she describes how

> man, proud man
> Dress'd in a little brief authority,
> Most ignorant of what he's most assur'd
> (His glassy essence), like an angry ape
> Plays such fantastic tricks before high heaven
> As makes the angels weep.
> (*Measure for Measure*, II. ii. 117–22)

The intellectual tricks that Faustus plays as 'he confounds hell in *Elizium*' (line 59) almost make the devil weep as he cries:

> O *Faustus*, leave these frivolous demaunds,
> Which strike a terror to my fainting soule. (lines 81–2)

This is the devil's own cry of despair, when he recognizes that the simple truths with which he has answered Faustus's questions about Lucifer, the fallen angels, and the reality of eternal damnation have had no effect on the doctor's resolution. The unexpectedly emotional appeal surprises even Faustus, but provokes only a sardonic comment:

> What, is great *Mephastophilis* so passionate,
> For being depriv'd of the joyes of heaven? (lines 83–4)

His determination now seems far stronger than it was at the beginning of the scene when, despite the excitement with which he embarked on his new experiment, he was forced to reassure himself: 'feare not *Faustus*, but be resolute' (line 14). The scene ends with his delighted 'speculation' as he waits for the midnight assignation and the exchange of contracts.

Ideologically this scene's significance lies in its demonstration that Faustus is in full possession of all the facts: he has been cautioned about the consequences that will ensue if he persists in his chosen action, and urged by Mephastophilis (surely the most powerful devil's advocate) to restrain his folly. He can now make no appeal on grounds of ignorance. There are, however, still more warnings to come. His conscience speaks, when he acknowledges that 'something soundeth in mine eares' persuading him to relinquish his new-found skills and 'turne to God againe' (scene 5); and even his own body revolts, withholding the blood that must write the contract. Faustus perceives the omen with dazzling clarity:

What might the staying of my bloud portend?
Is it unwilling I should write this bill?
Why streames it not, that I may write afresh?
Faustus gives to thee his soule: ah there it stayde,
Why shouldst thou not? is not thy soule thine owne? (scene 5 lines 64–8)

The tension mounts as Faustus, insisting on the freedom to pos-
sess his own soul, instantly commits it to Lucifer with the self-
conscious *Consummatum est*, the last words of Christ on the cross
(John 19: 30). A final warning comes when he hallucinates the 'inscription' on his arm: *Homo fuge*; and then the atmosphere relaxes
when Mephastophilis offers distraction—'Ile fetch him somewhat
to delight his minde'—with the dancing devils '*giving crownes and
rich apparell to* FAUSTUS'.

The relaxed interlude is a necessary preparation for the intense
solemnity of the episode that follows, in which verse gives way to
prose for the official exchange of contracts between Faustus and
Mephastophilis (acting as agent for Lucifer). When all the conditions have been iterated, the legalistic devil asks the formal question 'Speake *Faustus*, do you deliver this as your deede?' (scene 5
line 114). I suggest that here 'deede' has more than the superficial
sense of *OED* 4: 'an instrument in writing, purporting to effect
some legal disposition'; it has rather the import of *OED* 1: 'that
which is done, acted, or performed by an *intelligent or responsible
agent*'. The italics are mine.

The first soliloquy insists upon the intelligence of Faustus, and
the scenes that follow emphasize his responsibility. His response to
Mephastophilis' question about the 'deede', though apparently
flippant, seals his damnation: 'I, take it, and the divell give thee
good on't.'

The middle parts of the play are of doubtful authorship; nevertheless they present dramatically a classic case of mental and spiritual deterioration, the symptoms of which are soberly described
by William Perkins in his *Discourse of the Damned Art of Witchcraft* (1608):

When they first beginne to grow in confederacie with the deuill, they are
sober, and their understanding sound, they make their match waking,
and as they think wisely enough, knowing both what they promise the
deuill, and vpon what conditions, and therefore all this while it is no de-
lusion. But after they be once in the league, and haue been intangled in
compact with the deuill (considerately as they thinke, for their owne good

and aduantage) the case may be otherwise. For then reason and vnder-
standing may be depraued, memorie weakened and all the powers of their
soule blemished. Thus becoming his vassals they are deluded, and so
intoxicated by him that they will run into thousands of fantastical imagi-
nations, holding themselues to be transformed into the shapes of other
creatures, to be transported into the ayre into other countries, yes, to do
so many strange things which in truth they do not.

Perkins, who died in 1602, could almost be reporting a performance of *Dr Faustus*; although it is unlikely that so Calvinist a theologian would have had much time for the theatre—and would
certainly not have derived his doctrine from a play.

The first item of the infernal contract declares Faustus's damnation to the orthodox Christian: 'that Faustus may be a spirit in
form and substance'. For the Elizabethans 'spirit' had a variety of
meanings—Valdes and Cornelius appear to be referring to Para-
celsian elemental daemons, but when the remorseful Faustus is
told by the Evil Angel 'Thou art a spirite, God cannot pitty thee'
(scene 5, line 195), there is no doubt that 'spirite' is synonymous
with 'devil': Faustus must now be identified with the fallen angels
whom Mephastophilis had earlier described as:

> Unhappy spirits that fell with *Lucifer*,
> Conspir'd against our God with *Lucifer*,
> And are for ever damnd with *Lucifer*.
>   (scene 3 lines 70–2)

Medieval theology was quite clear about the fate of the fallen
angels: they were eternally damned, and could never achieve salvation. Renaissance theologians continued the doctrine—as we can
see from John Donne's explanation that:

To those that fell can appertain no reconciliation, no more then to those
that die in their sins; for *quod homini mors, Angelis casus*; The fall of the
Angels wrought upon them, as the death of a man does upon him.[8]

The play can only continue because the audience cannot be sure
(just as Faustus himself cannot be sure) how absolute is the signing
of the contract; and the Good Angel's reminder, which follows
Faustus's first disappointment with infernal resources, ensures
that the conflict in Faustus's mind (and consequently the tension

---

[8] John Donne, 'A Sermon Preached at St Paul's, upon Christmas Day. 1622', *The
Sermons of John Donne*, ed. G. R. Potter and E. M. Simpson (1959), iv. 299.

in the play) continues to the end: '*Faustus*, repent, yet God will pitty thee.' Faustus himself acknowledges the truth of this reminder: 'I God will pitty me, if I repent.' But the Evil Angel, typically, has the last word: 'I but *Faustus* never shal repent;' and Faustus is forced to acknowledge this truth too: 'My hearts so hardned I cannot repent' (scene 5 lines 194, 198, 199, 200). Then follows his confession of despair—a 'deepe dispaire' which tempts to suicide, but which is overcome with 'sweete pleasure'.

Shortly after this point Marlowe seems to have lost interest (temporarily) in his play; perhaps the triviality of the central section of his source narrative, *The English Faustbook*, bored him—or perhaps the problems of displaying superhuman knowledge (understandably) defeated him. Or it may be that his sudden death in 1593 left Henslowe with an unusual problem. But whether or not Marlowe intended to complete the middle portion of the play himself, it is certain that the writing at the end is his alone.

For the benefit of his academic friends, Faustus conjures up the famous Helen of Troy, 'that peerelesse Dame of *Greece*' (scene 12 line 6). When they see the apparition, the Scholars are speechless; they can only gasp with wonder:

> Too simple is my wit to tell her praise,
> Whom all the world admires for majestie. (lines 16–17)

Helen is a remarkably ambivalent figure—and not just in Marlowe's play. Her combination of absolute beauty and destructive potential was remarked by the Trojan Elders in the *Iliad* when Helen passed them as they sat, too old to join in the fighting, on one of the city towers, 'like cicadas perched on a tree in the woods, chirping delightfully'. As Helen approached the tower, they lowered their voices:

'Who on earth', they asked one another, 'could blame the Trojan and Achaean men-at-arms for suffering so long for such a woman's sake? Indeed, she is the very image of an immortal goddess. All the same, and lovely as she is, let her sail home and not stay here to vex us and our children after us.[9]

In Shakespeare's *Troilus and Cressida* Helen is the focus for argument amongst Trojans and Greeks; for the Trojan Troilus she is 'a

---

[9] *The Iliad*, III, trans. E. V. Rieu (1950).

theme of honour and renown, A spur to valiant and magnanimous deeds' (II. ii. 199–200). But later in the play the Greek Diomedes points out that

> For every false drop in her bawdy veins
> A Grecian's life has sunk; for every scruple
> Of her contaminated carrion weight
> A Troyan hath been slain. (IV. i. 71–4)

Marlowe is well aware of this ambivalence—as we appreciate with Helen's second appearance, after the Scholars have departed.

The apparition is not, of course, Helen herself. Faustus had done this kind of conjuring before, when he produced Alexander the Great and his Paramour for the entertainment of the German Emperor. On that occasion he prepared the spectators for the exhibition by explaining the nature of the illusion, admitting that 'it is not in my abilitie to present before your eyes, the true substantiall bodies of those two deceased princes which long since are consumed to dust' (scene 9 lines 43–6). He could, however, promise that 'such spirites as can lively resemble *Alexander* and his Paramour, shal appeare before your Grace, in that manner that they best liv'd in, in their most florishing estate' (lines 49–52). The scene is probably not Marlowe's own work—but the reminder is none the less useful, and so too is the warning that was added by the revisers of the B text when they told the Emperor not to address the apparitions, 'But in dumbe silence let them come and goe.' Similarly Faustus warns the Scholars that, when they see 'the admirablest Lady that ever lived', they should 'Be silent . . . for danger is in words' (scene 12 lines 14–15).

The first appearance of Helen *must* be exciting (and it certainly offers an enormous challenge to twentieth-century directors of *Dr Faustus*); but the audience should have recovered from its excitement by the time that the spirit is recalled, this time by Faustus himself with the expressed intent that her

> sweete imbracings may extinguish cleane
> These thoughts that do disswade me from my vow,
> And keepe mine oath I made to *Lucifer*. (lines 76–8)

The solemnity of her entrance in the early performance of the play can be inferred from the stage directions. Both texts ask for *Musicke* when she is presented to the Scholars, and both state that she *passeth over the Stage*—an unusual direction which, it has been suggested,[10] means that the character moves from one side of the yard, across the stage, and out at the other side of the yard, instead of entering by the stage doors. This would, of course, prolong the magic moment, which is received with the famous apostrophe to the 'face that lancht a thousand shippes'. As he declares his devotion, Faustus is elevated to the stature of a romantic hero, promising vigorous action in verse of soaring energy which comes to rest on Helen's lips: 'And then returne to *Helen* for a kisse' (line 93). The speech is a rapture of applause—for Helen herself, for the eternal beauty of form, for all that defies mortality. But it is more than this. As the delighted verse surges forward to praise what is lovely and enduring, an undertow drags back, recalling that such beauty brought destruction: a city was burnt, and topless towers laid in the dust. The two movements are balanced in a single couplet:

> Brighter art thou then flaming *Jupiter*,
> When he appeard to haplesse *Semele* (lines 96–7)

The sight of Jupiter in his divine majesty was more than mortal eyes could bear to look upon; and the 'haplesse *Semele*' was consumed by the brilliance. Faustus neglects his own warning to the Scholars, and embraces Helen with the neoplatonic lover's fancy: 'Her lips suckes forth my soule' (line 84). But his intended conceit is ironic reality if one accepts Greg's view that the kiss is a token act of intercourse, and that Faustus, convicted of demoniality, is now totally possessed by the devil. What the Scholars hailed as the 'onely Paragon of excellence' is in truth a succuba.[11]

The A text certainly insists that this episode is of major significance in the damnation of Faustus. An entrance is marked for the Old Man immediately after the kiss. The Old Man's first appearance in scene 12 showed him to be some kind of emissary from heaven, with a role comparable to that of Mercy in the medieval *Mankind* but with a human nature. He is a type of the true Christian, over whom the devil has no power, and Mephastophilis confesses diabolic impotence: 'His faith is great, I cannot touch his soule' (line 69). Although the verse of the Old Man's speech is

---

[10] See Allardyce Nicoll, 'Passing over the Stage', in *Shakespeare Survey*, XII (1959), 47 ff.

[11] W. W. Greg, 'The Damnation of Faustus', *Modern Language Review*, xli (1946), 97–107; reprinted in '*Dr Faustus*': *A Casebook*, ed. John Jump (1969), pp. 71–88.

unusually bad, his words have a powerful effect on Faustus, almost persuading him to repent with their vision of comfort:

> I see an Angell hovers ore thy head,
> And with a violl full of precious grace,
> Offers to powre the same into thy soule. (lines 44–7)

But what the Old Man witnesses in Faustus's courting of Helen is enough to make him give up hope:

> Accursed *Faustus*, miserable man,
> That from thy soule excludst the grace of heaven,
> And fliest the throne of his tribunall seate. (lines 101–3)

His meditation is interrupted by the tormenting devils, and his steadfast endurance of the physical suffering will serve later as a contrast to Faustus's inherent cowardice.

The B text omits this second appearance of the Old Man, and consequently loses the accurate diagnosis of Faustus's condition which is articulated in the Old Man's recognition that Faustus has closed his soul to 'the grace of heaven'. For the Christian, this explains Faustus's lament, much earlier in the play, that 'My hearts so hardned I cannot repent.' The situation which Faustus describes as he takes leave of the Scholars is expressed in the words of the Man of Despair, shut up in an iron cage, in Bunyan's *Pilgrim's Progress*:

I have grieved the Spirit, and he is gone; I tempted the Devil, and he is come to me; I have provoked God to Anger, and he has left me; I have so hardened my heart that I *cannot* repent.[12]

When the Scholars recommend that he should call on God, they learn of the state of despair in which Faustus has increasingly found himself; ever since he signed the infernal contract he has been unable either to weep or to pray:

I woulde weepe, but the divel drawes in my teares, gush foorth bloud, insteade of teares, yea life and soule, Oh he stayes my tong, I would lift up my hands, but see, they hold them, they hold them. (scene 13 lines 30–34)

Like Dido's grief at the realization of her love (*Dido Queene of Carthage*, III. iv. 25–30), the inarticulacy of the syntax makes for

---

[12] Part the First; my quotation is taken from an edition of 1882, p. 32.

eloquence; its formlessness in both cases utters the disorder of the speakers' emotions. Faustus is in an intolerable situation, but one that is not unfamiliar to Christian apologists. John Donne expressed the dilemma in the second of his Holy Sonnets, although the ease with which the poem resolves itself suggests that Donne's experience did not greatly trouble him:

> Yet grace, if thou repent, thou canst not lacke;
> But who shall give thee that grace to beginne?

Faustus can never find the 'grace to beginne'; his spasmodic efforts at repentance cannot withstand Mephastophilis's threats: 'the divell threatned to teare mee in peeces, if I namde God' (lines 45–6).

Faustus's condition can best be understood in terms of contemporary Christian doctrine. He has committed the one sin for which there is no forgiveness—the sin against the Holy Ghost. St Matthew's Gospel records Christ's teaching on the subject:

I say unto you. All manner of sin and blasphemy shall be forgiven unto men: but blasphemy against the Holy Ghost shall not be forgiven unto men.

And whosoever speaketh a word against the Son of Man, it shall be forgiven him: but whosoever speaketh against the Holy Ghost, it shall not be forgiven him, neither in this world, neither in the world to come. (12: 31–2)

The nature of the sin against the Holy Ghost is not defined in any of the Gospels, but Renaissance theologians followed the early Church Fathers in their teaching that pride and despair—two apparent opposites working in conjunction—could be so called. The 'Schoolemen', explained Donne, have noted certain sins:

Which they have called *sins against the Holy Ghost*, because naturally they shut out those meanes by which the Holy Ghost might work upon us. The first couple is, presumption and desperation; for presumption takes away the feare of God, and desperation the love of God . . . And truly . . . To presume upon God, that God cannot damne me eternally in the next world, for a fewe halfe houres in this . . . Or to despair, that God will not save me . . . al these are shrewd and slippery approaches towards the sin against the Holy Ghost.[13]

---

[13] 'A Sermon Preached upon Whitsunday', ?1623, *The Sermons of John Donne*, v. 93–4; see also Helen Gardner, 'The Theme of Damnation in *Dr Faustus*', in '*Dr Faustus*': *A Casebook*, ed. John Jump (1969), pp. 95–100.

The pride of Dr Faustus is evident from the very beginning of the play; even before the action starts, the Prologue describes him as being 'swolne with cunning of a selfe conceit', and Icarus is invoked as the type of uncontrolled ambition whose destruction Faustus must share since he shares the aspiration. And despair is present in his mind even before the contract is drawn up; as he meditates in his study before the appointment with Mephastophilis, he questions:

> Now *Faustus* must thou needes be damnd,
> And canst thou not be saved? (scene 5 lines 1–2)

His decision then was to 'Despair in God'; and during the course of the play his despair increases as his pride diminishes.

The sixteenth-century theologian Augustine Marlorat emphasized another quality which seems to have been, for him, a *sine qua non* for committing the sin against the Holy Ghost: the sinner must know what he is doing. According to Marlorat,

when a man is so touched with the light of the troth that he cannot pretend ignorance, and nevertheless of determinate malice resisteth, then he sinneth against the holy Ghost, and it is not possible for him to be reneued by repentance, in that he hath forsaken God.[14]

Marlowe's Dr Faustus 'cannot pretend ignorance'—unless the B text addition is allowed to take responsibility away from him at the last moment, and rob him also of his individuality and tragic stature.

The last soliloquy reverses the first. The proud scholar who had fretted at the restrictions imposed by the human condition and longed for the immortality of a god now seeks to avoid an eternity of damnation. Like a trapped animal, he lashes out against the mesh he has woven for himself; and becomes more entangled. To be physically absorbed by the elements, to be 'a creature wanting soule', 'some brutish beast'—even, at the last, to be no more than 'little water drops'—such is the last hope of the man who had (by his own account) 'Graveld the Pastors of the *Germaine* Church (scene 1 line 113). Time is the dominant in this speech. The measured regularity of the opening lines gives way to a frantic tugging in two directions as Faustus is torn between Christ and Lucifer:

---

[14] Augustine Marlorat, *A treatise of the Sin Against the Holy Ghost* (1570), f. A iv[r].

O Ile leape up to my God: who pulles me downe? (line 73)

The pace and the passion increase as the clock strikes relentlessly, and the second half-hour passes more quickly than the first. We are agonizingly aware of the last minutes of Faustus's life, trickling through the hour-glass with what seems like ever-increasing speed. But as each grain falls, bringing Faustus closer to his terrible end, we become more and more conscious of the deserts of vast eternity and damnation that open up beyond death.

When Macbeth and Lear die, the tragedies are ended with a final harmonious chord; the discords of Faustus's last speech cannot be easily resolved. Marlowe seems to have set himself to examine the question posed in the Gospel According to St Mark (8: 36): 'What shall it profit a man, if he shall gain the whole world, and lose his own soul?'

THE
TRAGICALL
History of D. Faustus.

As it hath bene Acted by the Right
Honorable the Earle of Nottingham his seruants.

Written by Ch. Marl.

LONDON
Printed by V. S. for Thomas Bushell. 1604.

Dramatis Personae

There is no list of Dramatis Personae in the A text, and any attempt to create one is likely to complicate more than it clarifies. The episodic nature of the play, together with the stereotypical characterization of all but the major *personae*, allows for maximum 'doubling' of the minor parts. The practice of modern theatre programmes is followed here, and the characters are listed 'in order of appearance'.

Chorus
Dr John Faustus
Wagner
Good Angel
Evil Angel
Valdes
Cornelius
Two Scholars
Mephastophilis
Clown
Lucifer
Belzebub
Seven Deadly Sins
   Pride
   Covetousness
   Wrath
   Envy
   Gluttony

   Sloth
   Lechery
Robin
Rafe
Pope
Cardinal of Lorraine
Friars
Vintner
Emperor of Germany
Knight
Horse-courser
Duke of Vanholt
Duchess of Vanholt
Third Scholar
Old Man
Attendants *and Spirits presenting* Alexander the Great, his Paramour, and Helen of Troy

The tragicall Historie
of Doctor Faustus

[Prologue]

Enter CHORUS.

Not marching now in fields of *Thracimene*,
Where *Mars* did mate the *Carthaginians*,
Nor sporting in the dalliance of love,
In courts of Kings where state is overturnd,
Nor in the pompe of prowd audacious deedes,   5
Intends our Muse to vaunt his heavenly verse:
Onely this (Gentlemen) we must performe,
The forme of *Faustus* fortunes good or bad.
To patient Judgements we appeale our plaude,
And speake for *Faustus* in his infancie: 10
Now is he borne, his parents base of stocke,
In *Germany*, within a towne calld *Rhodes*:
Of riper yeeres to *Wertenberg* he went,
Whereas his kinsmen chiefly brought him up,
So soone hee profites in Divinitie,   15
The fruitfull plot of Scholerisme grac't,
That shortly he was grac't with Doctors name,
Excelling all, whose sweete delight disputes
In heavenly matters of Theologie,
Till swolne with cunning of a selfe conceit,   20
His waxen wings did mount above his reach,
And melting heavens conspirde his overthrow.
For falling to a divelish exercise,
And glutted more with learnings golden gifts,
He surffets upon cursed Negromancy,   25
Nothing so sweete as magicke is to him
Which he preferres before his chiefest blisse,
And this the man that in his study sits.   *Exit.*

6 vaunt] *B*; daunt *A*

[Scene 1]

Enter FAUSTUS *in his Study.*

FAUSTUS. Settle thy studies *Faustus*, and beginne
To sound the deapth of that thou wilt professe:
Having commencde, be a Divine in shew,
Yet levell at the end of every Art,
And live and die in *Aristotles* workes: 5
Sweete *Analutikes* tis thou hast ravisht me,
Bene disserere est finis logicis,
Is, to dispute well, Logickes chiefest end
Affoords this Art no greater myracle:
Then reade no more, thou hast attaind the end: 10
A greater subject fitteth *Faustus* wit,
Bid *Oncaymaeon* farewell, *Galen* come:
Seeing, *ubi desinit philosophus, ibi incipit medicus.*
Be a physition *Faustus*, heape up golde,
And be eternizde for some wondrous cure,   15
Summum bonum medicinae sanitas,
The end of physicke is our bodies health:
Why *Faustus*, hast thou not attaind that end?
Is not thy common talke found Aphorismes?
Are not thy billes hung up as monuments,   20
Whereby whole Citties have escapt the plague,
And thousand desprate maladies beene easde,
Yet art thou still but *Faustus*, and a man.
Couldst thou make men to live eternally?
Or being dead, raise them to life againe?   25
Then this profession were to be esteemd.
Physicke farewell, where is *Justinian*?
Si una eademque res legatus duobus,
Alter rem alter valorem rei, &c.
A pretty case of paltry legacies: 30
Ex haereditari filium non potest pater nisi:
Such is the subject of the institute
And universall body of the law:

This study fittes a mercenary drudge,
Who aimes at nothing but externall trash,   35
Too servile and illiberall for me:
When all is done, Divinitie is best.
Jeromes Bible, *Faustus*, view it well.
Stipendium peccati mors est: ha, *Stipendium, &c.*
The reward of sinne is death: thats hard.   40
Si peccasse negamus, fallimur, & nulla est in nobis veritas.
If we say that we have no sinne,
We deceive our selves, and theres no truth in us.
Why then belike we must sinne,
And so consequently die.   45
I, we must die an everlasting death:
What doctrine call you this, *Che sera, sera,*
What wil be, shall be? Divinitie, adieu,
These Metaphisickes of Magicians,
And Negromantike bookes are heavenly   50
Lines, circles, schemes, letters and characters:
I, these are those that *Faustus* most desires.
O what a world of profit and delight,
Of power, of honor, of omnipotence
Is promised to the studious Artizan?   55
All things that moove betweene the quiet poles
Shalbe at my commaund, Emperours and Kings,
Are but obeyd in their severall provinces:
Nor can they raise the winde, or rend the cloudes:
But his dominion that exceedes in this,   60
Stretcheth as farre as doth the minde of man.
A sound Magician is a mighty god:
Heere *Faustus* trie thy braines to gaine a deitie.

Enter WAGNER.

Wagner, commend me to my deerest friends,
The *Germaine Valdes*, and *Cornelius*,   65
Request them earnestly to visite me.
WAGNER. I wil sir.   *exit.*
FAUSTUS. Their conference will be a greater help to me,
Then all my labours, plodde I nere so fast.

34 This] *B*; His *A*   36 Too servile] *B*; The devil *A*   51 schemes] sceanes
A; om. *B*

Enter the GOOD ANGELL *and the* EVILL ANGELL.

GOOD ANGEL. O *Faustus*, lay that damned booke aside,   70
 And gaze not on it, lest it tempt thy soule,
 And heape Gods heavy wrath upon thy head,
 Reade, reade the scriptures, that is blasphemy.
EVIL ANGEL. Go forward *Faustus* in that famous art,
 Wherein all natures treasury is contain'd: 75
 Be thou on earth as *Jove* is in the skie,
 Lord and commaunder of these Elements.   *Exeunt.*
FAUSTUS. How am I glutted with conceit of this?
 Shall I make spirits fetch me what I please,
 Resolve me of all ambiguities,   80
 Performe what desperate enterprise I will?
 Ile have them flye to *India* for gold,
 Ransacke the Ocean for orient pearle,
 And search all corners of the new found world
 For pleasant fruites and princely delicates: 85
 Ile have them reade mee straunge philosophie,
 And tell the secrets of all forraine kings,
 Ile have them wall all *Jermany* with brasse,
 And make swift *Rhine* circle faire *Wertenberge*,
 Ile have them fill the publike schooles with silk,   90
 Wherewith the students shalbe bravely clad:
 Ile levy souldiers with the coyne they bring,
 And chase the Prince of *Parma* from our land,
 And raigne sole king of all our provinces:
 Yea stranger engines for the brunt of warre,   95
 Then was the fiery keele at *Antwarpes* bridge,
 Ile make my servile spirits to invent:
 Come *Germaine Valdes* and *Cornelius*,
 And make me blest with your sage conference,
 Valdes, sweete *Valdes*, and *Cornelius*,   100

Enter VALDES *and* CORNELIUS.

Know that your words have woon me at the last,
 To practise Magicke and concealed arts:
 Yet not your words onely, but mine owne fantasie,
 That will receive no object for my head,

90 silk] *Dyce*; skill *A*

But ruminates on Negromantique skill,   105
Philosophy is odious and obscure,
Both Law and Phisicke are for pettie wits,
Divinitie is basest of the three,
Unpleasant, harsh, contemptible and vilde,
Tis Magicke, Magicke that hath ravisht mee,   110
Then gentle friends ayde me in this attempt,
And I that have with Consis sylogismes
Graveld the Pastors of the *Germaine* Church,
And made the flowring pride of *Wertenberge*
Swarme to my Problemes as the infernall spirits   115
On sweet *Musaeus* when he came to hell,
Will be as cunning as *Agrippa* was,
Whose shadowes made all *Europe* honor him.

VALDES. *Faustus* these bookes thy wit and our experience
    Shall make all nations to canonize us,   120
    As *Indian* Moores obey their *Spanish* Lords,
    So shall the spirits of every element
    Be alwaies serviceable to us three,
    Like Lyons shall they guard us when we please,
    Like *Almaine* Rutters with their horsemens staves,   125
    Or *Lapland* Gyants trotting by our sides,
    Sometimes like women, or unwedded maides,
    Shadowing more beautie in their ayrie browes,
    Then in the white breasts of the queene of Love:
    From *Venice* shall they dragge huge Argoces,   130
    And from *America* the golden fleece,
    That yearely stuffes olde *Philips* treasury
    If learned *Faustus* will be resolute.

FAUSTUS. *Valdes* as resolute am I in this
    As thou to live, therefore object it not.   135

CORNELIUS. The myracles that Magicke will performe,
    Will make thee vow to studie nothing else,
    He that is grounded in Astrologie,
    Inricht with tongues well seene in minerals,
    Hath all the principles Magicke doth require,   140
    Then doubt not (*Faustus*) but to be renowmd,
    And more frequented for this mystery,

122 spirits] *B*; subjects *A*   129 the white] *Greg*; their white *A*   130 From]
*A*2; For *A*1   139 seene in minerals] *A*2; ~∧~ *A*1

Then heretofore the *Delphian* Oracle.
The spirits tell me they can drie the sea,
And fetch the treasure of all forraine wrackes, 145
I, all the wealth that our forefathers hid
Within the massie entrailes of the earth.
Then tell me *Faustus*, what shal we three want?
FAUSTUS. Nothing *Cornelius*, O this cheares my soule,
Come shewe me some demonstrations magicall, 150
That I may conjure in some lustie grove,
And have these joyes in full possession.
VALDES. Then haste thee to some solitary grove,
And beare wise *Bacons* and *Albanus* workes,
The Hebrew Psalter, and new Testament, 155
And whatsoever else is requisit
Wee will enforme thee ere our conference cease.
CORNELIUS. *Valdes*, first let him know the words of art,
And then all other ceremonies learnd,
Faustus may trie his cunning by himselfe. 160
VALDES. First Ile instruct thee in the rudiments,
And then wilt thou be perfecter then I.
FAUSTUS. Then come and dyne with me, and after meate
Weele canvas every quidditie thereof:
For ere I sleepe Ile trie what I can do, 165
This night Ile conjure though I die therefore. *Exeunt.*

[Scene 2]

Enter two SCHOLLERS.

1 SCHOLAR. I wonder whats become of *Faustus*, that was
wont to make our schooles ring with, *sic probo*.
2 SCHOLAR. That shall we know, for see here comes his boy.

Enter WAGNER.

1 SCHOLAR. How now sirra, wheres thy maister?
WAGNER. God in heaven knowes. 5
2 SCHOLAR. Why, dost not thou know?
WAGNER. Yes I know, but that followes not.

1 SCHOLAR. Go too sirra, leave your jeasting, and tell us
    where hee is.
WAGNER. That follows not necessary by force of argument,   10
    that you being licentiats should stand upon't, therefore
    acknowledge your error, and be attentive.
2 SCHOLAR. Why, didst thou not say thou knewst?
WAGNER. Have you any witnesse on't?
1 SCHOLAR. Yes sirra, I heard you.   15
WAGNER. Aske my fellow if I be a thiefe.
2 SCHOLAR. Well, you will not tell us.
WAGNER. Yes sir, I will tell you, yet if you were not dunces
    you would never aske me such a question, for is not he
    corpus naturale, and is not that *mobile*, then wherefore   20
    should you aske me such a question: but that I am by nature
    flegmaticke, slowe to wrath, and prone to leachery, (to love I
    would say) it were not for you to come within fortie foote of
    the place of execution, although I do not doubt to see you
    both hang'd the next Sessions. Thus having triumpht over   25
    you, I will set my countnance like a precisian, and begin to
    speake thus: truly my deare brethren, my maister is within
    at dinner with *Valdes* and *Cornelius*, as this wine if it could
    speake, it would enforme your worships, and so the Lord
    blesse you, preserve you, and keepe you my deare brethren,   30
    my deare brethren.   *Exit*.
1 SCHOLAR. Nay then I feare he is falne into that damned
    art, for which they two are infamous through the world.
2 SCHOLAR. Were he a stranger, and not alied to me, yet
    should I grieve for him: but come let us go and informe the   35
    Rector, and see if hee by his grave counsaile can reclaime
    him.
1 SCHOLAR. O but I feare me nothing can reclaime him.
2 SCHOLAR. Yet let us trie what we can do.   *Exeunt*.

[Scene 3]

Enter FAUSTUS *to conjure.*

FAUSTUS. Now that the gloomy shadow of the earth,
Longing to view *Orions* drisling looke,
Leapes from th'antartike world unto the skie,
And dimmes the welkin with her pitchy breath:
Faustus, begin thine incantations,   5
And trie if divels will obey thy hest,
Seeing thou hast prayde and sacrific'd to them.
Within this circle is *Jehovahs* name,
Forward and backward, Anagramatis'd,
The breviated names of holy Saints,   10
Figures of every adjunct to the heavens,
And characters of signes and erring starres,
By which the spirits are inforst to rise.
Then feare not *Faustus*, but be resolute,
And trie the uttermost Magicke can performe.   15
Sint mihi dei acherontis propitii, valeat numen triplex Jehovae,
ignei, aerii, Aquatani spiritus salvete, Orientis princeps, Belsi-
bub inferni ardentis monarcha & demigorgon, propitiamus vos,
ut apariat & surgat Mephastophilis, quid tu moraris, per
Jehovam gehennam & consecratam aquam quam nunc spargo,   20
signumque crucis quod nunc facio, & per vota nostra ipse
nunc surgat nobis dicatis Mephastophilis.

Enter a Divell.

I charge thee to returne and chaunge thy shape,
Thou art too ugly to attend on me,
Goe and returne an old Franciscan Frier,   25
That holy shape becomes a divell best.   *Exit divell.*
I see theres vertue in my heavenly words,
Who would not be proficient in this art?
How pliant is this *Mephastophilis*?
Full of obedience and humilitie,   30
Such is the force of Magicke and my spels,

9 Anagramatis'd] *B*; and Agramithist *A*   19 *quid tu moraris*] *Boas*; *quod tumeraris A*

No *Faustus*, thou art Conjurer laureate
That canst commaund great *Mephastophilis*,
Quin redis Mephastophilis fratris imagine.

Enter MEPHOSTOPHILIS.

MEPHASTOPHILIS. Now *Faustus*, what wouldst thou have
    me do?   35
FAUSTUS. I charge thee wait upon me whilst I live,
    To do what ever *Faustus* shall commaund,
    Be it to make the Moone drop from her spheare,
    Or the Ocean to overwhelme the world.
MEPHASTOPHILIS. I am a servant to great *Lucifer*,   40
    And may not follow thee without his leave,
    No more then he commaunds must we performe.
FAUSTUS. Did not he charge thee to appeare to mee?
MEPHASTOPHILIS. No, I came now hither of mine owne
    accord.
FAUSTUS. Did not my conjuring speeches raise thee? speake.   45
MEPHASTOPHILIS. That was the cause, but yet *per accident*,
    For when we heare one racke the name of God,
    Abjure the scriptures, and his Saviour *Christ*,
    Wee flye, in hope to get his glorious soule,
    Nor will we come, unlesse he use such meanes   50
    Whereby he is in danger to be damnd:
    Therefore the shortest cut for conjuring
    Is stoutly to abjure the Trinitie,
    And pray devoutly to the prince of hell.
FAUSTUS. So *Faustus* hath already done, & holds this prin-
    ciple,   55
    There is no chiefe but only *Belsibub*,
    To whom *Faustus* doth dedicate himselfe,
    This word damnation terrifies not him,
    For he confounds hell in *Elizium*,
    His ghost be with the olde Philosophers,   60
    But leaving these vaine trifles of mens soules,
    Tell me what is that *Lucifer* thy Lord?
MEPHASTOPHILIS. Arch-regent and commaunder of all
    spirits.

34 *redis*] Boas; *regis A*

FAUSTUS. Was not that *Lucifer* an Angell once?
MEPHASTOPHILIS. Yes *Faustus*, and most dearely lov'd of
   God.   65
FAUSTUS. How comes it then that he is prince of divels?
MEPHASTOPHILIS. O by aspiring pride and insolence,
   For which God threw him from the face of heaven.
FAUSTUS. And what are you that live with *Lucifer*?
MEPHASTOPHILIS. Unhappy spirits that fell with *Lucifer*,   70
   Conspir'd against our God with *Lucifer*,
   And are for ever damnd with *Lucifer*.
FAUSTUS. Where are you damn'd?
MEPHASTOPHILIS. In hell.
FAUSTUS. How comes it then that thou art out of hel?   75
MEPHASTOPHILIS. Why this is hel, nor am I out of it:
   Thinkst thou that I who saw the face of God,
   And tasted the eternal joyes of heaven,
   Am not tormented with ten thousand hels,
   In being depriv'd of everlasting blisse: 80
   O *Faustus*, leave these frivolous demaunds,
   Which strike a terror to my fainting soule.
FAUSTUS. What, is great *Mephastophilis* so passionate,
   For being deprivd of the joyes of heaven?
   Learne thou of *Faustus* manly fortitude,   85
   And scorne those joyes thou never shalt possesse.
   Go beare these tidings to great *Lucifer*,
   Seeing *Faustus* hath incurrd eternall death,
   By desprate thoughts against *Joves* deitie:
   Say, he surrenders up to him his soule,   90
   So he will spare him foure and twentie yeeres,
   Letting him live in al voluptuousnesse,
   Having thee ever to attend on me,
   To give me whatsoever I shal aske,
   To tel me whatsoever I demaund,   95
   To slay mine enemies, and ayde my friends,
   And always be obedient to my wil:
   Goe and returne to mighty *Lucifer*,
   And meete mee in my study at midnight,
   And then resolve me of thy maisters minde.   100

87 *these*] *B*; those *A*

MEPHASTOPHILIS. I will *Faustus*.   *exit.*
FAUSTUS. Had I as many soules as there be starres,
    Ide give them al for *Mephastophilis*:
    By him Ile be great Emprour of the world,
    And make a bridge through the mooving ayre,   105
    To passe the Ocean with a band of men,
    Ile joyne the hils that binde the *Affricke* shore,
    And make that land continent to *Spaine*,
    And both contributory to my crowne:
    The Emprour shal not live but by my leave,   110
    Nor any Potentate of *Germany*:
    Now that I have obtaind what I desire,
    Ile live in speculation of this Art,
    Til *Mephastophilis* returne againe.   *exit.*

[Scene 4]

Enter WAGNER *and the* CLOWNE.

WAGNER. Sirra boy, come hither.
CLOWN. How, boy? swowns boy, I hope you have seene
    many boyes with such pickadevaunts as I have. Boy quotha?
WAGNER. Tel me sirra, hast thou any commings in?
CLOWN. I, and goings out too, you may see else.   5
WAGNER. Alas poore slave, see how poverty jesteth in his
    nakednesse, the vilaine is bare, and out of service, and so
    hungry, that I know he would give his soule to the Divel for
    a shoulder of mutton, though it were blood rawe.
CLOWN. How, my soule to the Divel for a shoulder of   10
    mutton though twere blood rawe? not so good friend,
    burladie I had neede have it wel roasted, and good sawce to
    it, if I pay so deere.
WAGNER. Wel, wilt thou serve me, and Ile make thee go like
    Qui mihi discipulus?   15
CLOWN. How, in verse?
WAGNER. No, sirra, in beaten silke and staves acre.
CLOWN. How, how knaves acre? I, I thought that was al the

land his father left him: Doe yee heare, I would be sorie to
robbe you of your living.   20

WAGNER. Sirra, I say in staves acre.

CLOWN. Oho, oho, staves acre, why then belike, if I were
your man, I should be ful of vermine.

WAGNER. So thou shalt, whether thou beest with me, or no:
but sirra, leave your jesting, and binde your selfe presently   25
unto me for seaven yeeres, or Ile turne al the lice about thee
into familiars, and they shal teare thee in peeces.

CLOWN. Doe you heare sir? you may save that labour, they
are too familiar with me already, swowns they are as bolde
with my flesh, as if they had payd for my meate and drinke.   30

WAGNER. Wel, do you heare sirra? holde, take these gilders.

CLOWN. Gridyrons, what be they?

WAGNER. Why *french* crownes.

CLOWN. Mas but for the name of *french* crownes a man were
as good have as many *english* counters, and what should I do   35
with these?

WAGNER. Why now sirra thou art at an houres warning
whensoever or wheresoever the divell shall fetch thee.

CLOWN. No, no, here take your gridirons againe.

WAGNER. Truly Ile none of them.   40

CLOWN. Truly but you shall.

WAGNER. Beare witnesse I gave them him.

CLOWN. Beare witnesse I give them you againe.

WAGNER. Well, I will cause two divels presently to fetch
thee away *Baliol* and *Belcher*.   45

CLOWN. Let your *Balio* and your *Belcher* come here, and Ile
knocke them, they were never so knockt since they were
divels, say I should kill one of them, what would folkes say?
do ye see yonder tall fellow in the round slop, hee has kild
the divell, so I should be cald kill divell all the parish over.   50

Enter two divells, and the CLOWNE *runnes up and downe crying.*

WAGNER. *Baliol* and *Belcher*, spirits away.   *Exeunt.*

CLOWN. What, are they gone? a vengeance on them, they
have vilde long nailes, there was a hee divell and a shee
divell, Ile tell you how you shall know them, all hee divels
has hornes, and all shee divels has clifts and cloven feete.   55

WAGNER. Well sirra follow me.

CLOWN. But do you hear? if I should serve you, would you
    teach me to raise up *Banios* and *Belcheos*?
WAGNER. I will teach thee to turne thy selfe to anything, to a
    dogge, or a catte, or a mouse, or a ratte, or any thing.   60
CLOWN. How? a Christian fellow to a dogge or a catte, a
    mouse or a ratte? no, no sir, if you turne me into any thing,
    let it be in the likenesse of a little pretie frisking flea, that I
    may be here and there and every where, O Ile tickle the
    pretie wenches plackets Ile be amongst them ifaith.   65
WAGNER. Wel sirra, come.
CLOWN. But doe you heare *Wagner*?
WAGNER. How *Balioll* and *Belcher*.
CLOWN. O Lord I pray sir, let *Banio* and *Belcher* go sleepe.
WAGNER. Vilaine, call me Maister *Wagner*, and let thy left   70
    eye be diametarily fixt vpon my right heele, with *quasi*
    vestigias nostras insistere.   *exit.*
CLOWN. God forgive me, he speakes *Dutch* fustian: well, Ile
    folow him, Ile serve him, thats flat.   *exit.*

[Scene 5]

Enter FAUSTUS *in his Study*.

FAUSTUS. Now *Faustus* must thou needes be damnd,
    And canst thou not be saved?
    What bootes it then to thinke of God or heaven?
    Away with such vaine fancies and despaire,
    Despaire in God, and trust in *Belsabub*:   5
    Now go not backeward: no *Faustus*, be resolute,
    Why waverest thou? O something soundeth in mine eares:
    Abjure this Magicke, turne to God againe,
    I and *Faustus* wil turne to God againe.
    To God? he loves thee not,   10
    The god thou servest is thine owne appetite,
    Wherein is fixt the love of *Belsabub*,
    To him Ile build an altare and a church,
    And offer luke warme blood of new borne babes.

Enter GOOD ANGELL, *and* EVILL.

GOOD ANGEL. Sweet *Faustus*, leave that execrable art.   15
FAUSTUS. Contrition, prayer, repentance: what of them?
GOOD ANGEL. O they are meanes to bring thee unto heaven.
EVIL ANGEL. Rather illusions fruites of lunacy,
    That makes men foolish that do trust them most.
GOOD ANGEL. Sweet *Faustus* thinke of heaven, and
    heavenly things.   20
EVIL ANGEL. No *Faustus*, thinke of honor and of wealth.
                  exeunt [ANGELLS].
FAUSTUS. Of wealth,
    Why the signory of *Emden* shalbe mine,
    When *Mephastophilus* shal stand by me,
    What God can hurt thee *Faustus*? thou art safe,   25
    Cast no more doubts, come *Mephastophilus*,
    And bring glad tidings from great *Lucifer*:
    Ist not midnight? come *Mephastophilus*,
    Veni veni Mephastophile

Enter MEPH:

    Now tel, what sayes *Lucifer* thy Lorde?   30
MEPHASTOPHILIS. That I shal waite on *Faustus* whilst he
    lives,
    So he wil buy my service with his soule.
FAUSTUS. Already *Faustus* hath hazarded that for thee.
MEPHASTOPHILIS. But *Faustus*, thou must bequeathe it
    solemnely,
    And write a deede of gift with thine owne blood,   35
    For that security craves great *Lucifer*:
    If thou deny it, I wil backe to hel.
FAUSTUS. Stay *Mephastophilus*, and tel me, what good wil
    my soule do thy Lord?
MEPHASTOPHILIS. Inlarge his kingdome.   40
FAUSTUS. Is that the reason he tempts us thus?
MEPHASTOPHILIS. *Solamen miseris socios habuisse doloris.*
FAUSTUS. Have you any paine that torture others?
MEPHASTOPHILIS. As great as have the humane soules of
    men:

   21 and of wealth] *A2*; ~ ∧ ~ *A1*   31 he lives] *B*; I live *A*   43 torture] *B*;
tortures *A*

But tel me *Faustus*, shal I have thy soule,   45
And I wil be thy slave, and waite on thee,
And give thee more than thou hast wit to aske.
FAUSTUS. I *Mephastophilus*, I give it thee.
MEPHASTOPHILIS. Then stabbe thine arme couragiously,
And binde thy soule, that at some certaine day   50
Great *Lucifer* may claime it as his owne,
And then be thou as great as *Lucifer*.
FAUSTUS. Loe *Mephastophilus*, for love of thee,
I cut mine arme, and with my proper blocd
Assure my soule to be great *Lucifers*,   55
Chiefe Lord and regent of perpetual night,
View heere the blood that trickles from mine arme,
And let it be propitious for my wish.
MEPHASTOPHILIS. But *Faustus*, thou must write it in
manner of a deede of gift.   60
FAUSTUS. I so I will, but *Mephastophilis*
My bloud conjeales and I can write no more.
MEPHASTOPHILIS. Ile fetch thee fier to dissolve it straight.
Exit.

FAUSTUS. What might the staying of my bloud portend?
Is it unwilling I should write this bill?   65
Why streames it not, that I may write afresh?
Faustus gives to thee his soule: ah there it stayde,
Why shouldst thou not? is not thy soule thine owne?
Then write againe, *Faustus* gives to thee his soule.

Enter MEPHASTOPHILIS *with a chafer of coles.*

MEPHASTOPHILIS. Heres fier, come *Faustus*, set it on.   70
FAUSTUS. So now the bloud begins to cleare againe,
Now will I make an ende immediately.
MEPHASTOPHILIS. O what will not I do to obtaine his
soule?
FAUSTUS. *Consummatum est*, this Bill is ended,
And *Faustus* hath bequeath'd his soule to *Lucifer*.   75
But what is this inscription on mine arme?
Homo fuge, whither should I flie?
If unto God hee'le throwe thee downe to hell,
My sences are deceiv'd, here's nothing writ,
I see it plaine, here in this place is writ,   80

Homo fuge, yet shall not *Faustus* flye.
MEPHASTOPHILIS. Ile fetch him somewhat to delight his
  minde.   *exit.*

> *Enter with divels, giving crownes and rich apparell to*
> FAUSTUS, *and daunce, and then depart.*

FAUSTUS. Speake *Mephastophilis*, what meanes this shewe?
MEPHASTOPHILIS. Nothing *Faustus*, but to delight thy
  minde withall,
  And to shewe thee what Magicke can performe.   85
FAUSTUS. But may I raise up spirits when I please?
MEPHASTOPHILIS. I *Faustus*, and do greater things then
  these.
FAUSTUS. Then theres inough for a thousand soules,
  Here *Mephastophilis* receive this scrowle,
  A deede of gift of body and of soule: 90
  But yet conditionally, that thou performe
  All articles prescrib'd betweene us both.
MEPHASTOPHILIS. *Faustus*, I sweare by hel and *Lucifer*
  To effect all promises betweene us made.
FAUSTUS. Then heare me read them: on these conditions   95
  following.
    First, that *Faustus* may be a spirit in forme and sub-
  stance.
    Secondly, that *Mephastophilis* shall be his servant, and at
  his commaund.   100
    Thirdly, that *Mephastophilis* shall do for him, and bring
  him whatsoever.
    Fourthly, that hee shall be in his chamber or house
  invisible.
    Lastly, that hee shall appeare to the said *John Faustus* at 105
  all times, in what forme or shape soever he please.
  I *John Faustus* of *Wertenberge*, Doctor, by these presents, do
  give both body and soule to *Lucifer* prince of the East, and
  his minister *Mephastophilis*, and furthermore graunt unto
  them, that foure and twentie yeares being expired, the 110
  articles above written inviolate, full power to fetch or carry
  the said *John Faustus* body and soule, flesh, bloud, or goods,
  into their habitation wheresoever.   *By me John Faustus.*

MEPHASTOPHILIS. Speake *Faustus*, do you deliver this as
    your deede? 115
FAUSTUS. I, take it, and the divell give thee good on't.
MEPHASTOPHILIS. Now *Faustus* aske what thou wilt.
FAUSTUS. First will I question with thee about hell,
    Tel me, where is the place that men call hell?
MEPHASTOPHILIS. Under the heavens. 120
FAUSTUS. I, but where about?
MEPHASTOPHILIS. Within the bowels of these elements,
    Where we are tortur'd and remaine for ever,
    Hell hath no limits, nor is circumscrib'd
    In one selfe place, for where we are is hell, 125
    And where hell is, must we ever be:
    And to conclude, when all the world dissolves,
    And every creature shalbe purified,
    All places shall be hell that is not heaven.
FAUSTUS. Come, I thinke hell's a fable. 130
MEPHASTOPHILIS. I, thinke so still, till experience change
    thy minde.
FAUSTUS. Why? thinkst thou then that *Faustus* shall bee
    damn'd?
MEPHASTOPHILIS. I of necessitie, for here's the scrowle,
    Wherein thou hast given thy soule to *Lucifer*.
FAUSTUS. I, and body too, but what of that? 135
    Thinkst thou that *Faustus* is so fond,
    To imagine, that after this life there is any paine?
    Tush these are trifles and meere olde wives tales.
MEPHASTOPHILIS. But *Faustus* I am an instance to prove
    the contrary·
    For I am damnd, and am now in hell. 140
FAUSTUS. How? now in hell? nay and this be hell, Ile willingly
    be damnd here: what walking, disputing, &c. But leaving off
    this, let me have a wife, the fairest maid in *Germany*, for I am
    wanton and lascivious, and can not live without a wife.
MEPHASTOPHILIS. How, a wife? I prithee *Faustus* talke not 145
    of a wife.
FAUSTUS. Nay sweete *Mephastophilis* fetch me one, for I will
    have one.
MEPHASTOPHILIS. Well thou wilt have one, sit there till I
    come, Ile fetch thee a wife in the divels name. [*exit.*]

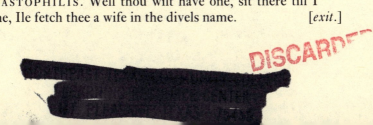

Enter with a divell drest like a woman,
with fier workes.

MEPHASTOPHILIS. Tell *Faustus*, how dost thou like thy
    wife?

FAUSTUS. A plague on her for a hote whore.

MEPHASTOPHILIS. Tut *Faustus*, marriage is but a cere-
    moniall toy, if thou lovest me, thinke no more of it.   155
    Ile cull thee out the fairest curtezans,
    And bring them ev'ry morning to thy bed,
    She whome thine eie shall like, thy heart shal have,
    Be she as chaste as was *Penelope*,
    As wise as *Saba*, or as beautiful   160
    As was bright *Lucifer* before his fall.
    Hold, take this booke, peruse it thorowly,
    The iterating of these lines brings golde,
    The framing of this circle on the ground,
    Brings whirlewindes, tempests, thunder and lightning.   165
    Pronounce this thrice devoutly to thy selfe,
    And men in armour shal appeare to thee,
    Ready to execute what thou desirst.

FAUSTUS. Thankes *Mephastophilus*, yet faine would I have a
    booke wherein I might beholde al spels and incantations,   170
    that I might raise up spirits when I please.

MEPHASTOPHILIS. Here they are in this booke.
                                                   There turne to them.

FAUSTUS. Now would I have a booke where I might see al
    characters and planets of the heavens, that I might knowe
    their motions and dispositions.   175

MEPHASTOPHILIS. Heere they are too.   *Turne to them.*

FAUSTUS. Nay let me have one booke more, and then I have
    done, wherein I might see al plants, hearbes and trees that
    grow upon the earth.

MEPHASTOPHILIS. Here they be.   180

FAUSTUS. O thou art deceived.

MEPHASTOPHILIS. Tut I warrant thee.   *Turne to them.*

FAUSTUS. When I behold the heavens, then I repent,
    And curse thee wicked *Mephastophilus*,
    Because thou hast depriv'd me of those joyes.

MEPHASTOPHILIS. Why *Faustus*,
  Thinkst thou heaven is such a glorious thing?
  I tel thee tis not halfe so faire as thou,
  Or any man that breathes on earth.
FAUSTUS. How proovest thou that?   190
MEPHASTOPHILIS. It was made for man, therefore is man
  more excellent.
FAUSTUS. If it were made for man, twas made for me:
  I wil renounce this magicke, and repent.

       Enter GOOD ANGEL, *and* EVILL ANGEL.

GOOD ANGEL. *Faustus*, repent, yet God will pitty thee.
EVIL ANGEL. Thou art a spirite, God cannot pitty thee.   195
FAUSTUS. Who buzzeth in mine eares I am a spirite?
  Be I a divel, yet God may pitty me,
  I God wil pitty me, if I repent.
EVIL ANGEL. I but *Faustus* never shal repent.
                         exeunt [ANGELLS].
FAUSTUS. My hearts so hardned I cannot repent,   200
  Scarse can I name salvation, faith, or heaven,
  But feareful ecchoes thunders in mine eares,
  Faustus, thou art damn'd, then swordes and knives,
  Poyson, gunnes, halters, and invenomd steele
  Are layde before me to dispatch my selfe,   205
  And long ere this I should have slaine my selfe,
  Had not sweete pleasure conquerd deepe dispaire.
  Have not I made blinde *Homer* sing to me,
  Of *Alexanders* love, and *Enons* death,
  And hath not he that built the walles of *Thebes*,   210
  With ravishing sound of his melodious harp
  Made musicke with my *Mephastophilis*,
  Why should I dye then, or basely dispaire?
  I am resolv'd *Faustus* shal nere repent,
  Come *Mephastophilis*, let us dispute againe,   215
  And argue of divine Astrologie,
  Tel me, are there many heavens above the Moone?
  Are all celestiall bodies but one globe,
 .As is the substance of this centricke earth?
MEPHASTOPHILIS. As are the elements, such are the
  spheares,   220

Mutually folded in each others orbe,
And *Faustus* all jointly move upon one axletree,
Whose termine is tearmd the worlds wide pole,
Nor are the names of *Saturne*, *Mars*, or *Jupiter*
Faind, but are erring starres. 225

FAUSTUS. But tell me, have they all one motion? both *situ &*
tempore.

MEPHASTOPHILIS. All joyntly move from East to West in
24. houres upon the poles of the world, but differ in their
motion upon the poles of the Zodiake. 230

FAUSTUS. Tush, these slender trifles *Wagner* can decide,
Hath *Mephastophilus* no greater skill?
Who knowes not the double motion of the plannets?
The first is finisht in a naturall day,
The second thus, as *Saturne* in 30. yeares, *Jupiter* in 12. *Mars* 235
in 4. the Sunne, *Venus*, and *Mercury* in a yeere: the Moone
in 28. dayes. Tush these are fresh mens suppositions, but
tell me hath every spheare a dominion or *Intelligentij*?

MEPHASTOPHILIS. I.

FAUSTUS. How many heavens or spheares are there? 240

MEPHASTOPHILIS. Nine, the seven planets, the firmament,
and the imperiall heaven.

FAUSTUS. Well, resolve me in this question, why have wee
not conjunctions, oppositions, aspects, eclipsis, all at one
time, but in some yeares we have more, in some lesse? 245

MEPHASTOPHILIS. *Per inaequalem motum respectu totius.*

FAUSTUS. Well, I am answered, tell me who made the
world?

MEPHASTOPHILIS. I will not.

FAUSTUS. Sweete *Mephastophilus* tell me. 250

MEPHASTOPHILIS. Move me not, for I will not tell thee.

FAUSTUS. Villaine, have I not bound thee to tel me any
thing?

MEPHASTOPHILIS. I, that is not against our kingdome, but
this is, 255
Thinke thou on hell *Faustus*, for thou art damnd.

FAUSTUS. Thinke *Faustus* upon God that made the world.

MEPHASTOPHILIS. Remember this. *Exit.*

FAUSTUS. I, goe accursed spirit to ugly hell,
Tis thou hast damn'd distressed *Faustus* soule: 260
Ist not too late?

Enter GOOD ANGELL *and* EVILL.

EVIL ANGEL. Too late.

GOOD ANGEL. Never too late, if *Faustus* can repent.

EVIL ANGEL. If thou repent divels shal teare thee in peeces.

GOOD ANGEL. Repent, & they shall never race thy skin.   265

Exeunt [ANGELLS].

FAUSTUS. Ah *Christ* my Saviour, seeke to save distressed
Faustus soule.

Enter LUCIFER, BELSABUB, *and* MEPHASTOPHILUS.

LUCIFER. *Christ* cannot save thy soule, for he is just,
   Theres none but I have intrest in the same.

FAUSTUS. O who art thou that lookst so terrible?

LUCIFER. I am *Lucifer*, and this is my companion Prince in
   hel.   270

FAUSTUS. O *Faustus*, they are come to fetch away thy soule.

LUCIFER. We come to tell thee thou dost injure us,
   Thou talkst of *Christ*, contrary to thy promise
   Thou shouldst not thinke of God, thinke of the devil,
   And of his dame too.   275

FAUSTUS. Nor will I henceforth: pardon me in this,
   And *Faustus* vowes never to looke to heaven,
   Never to name God, or to pray to him,
   To burne his Scriptures, slay his Ministers,
   And make my spirites pull his churches downe.   280

LUCIFER. Do so, and we will highly gratify thee: *Faustus*, we
   are come from hel to shew thee some pastime: sit downe,
   and thou shalt see al the seaven deadly sinnes appeare in
   their proper shapes.

FAUSTUS. That sight will be as pleasing unto me, as paradise 285
   was to *Adam*, the first day of his creation.

LUCIFER. Talke not of paradise, nor creation, but marke this
   shew, talke of the divel, and nothing else: come away.

Enter the seaven deadly SINNES.

Now *Faustus*, examine them of their several names and dis-
positions.   290

FAUSTUS. What art thou? the first.

PRIDE. I am *Pride*, I disdaine to have any parents, I am like
   to *Ovids* flea, I can creepe into every corner of a wench,

sometimes like a periwig, I sit upon her brow, or like a fan
of feathers, I kisse her lippes, indeede I doe, what doe I not? 295
but fie, what a scent is here? Ile not speake an other worde,
except the ground were perfumde and covered with cloth of
arras.

FAUSTUS. What art thou? the second.

COVETOUSNESS. I am *Covetousnes*, begotten of an olde 300
churle, in an olde leatherne bag: and might I have my wish,
I would desire, that this house, and all the people in it were
turnd to golde, that I might locke you uppe in my good
chest, O my sweete golde.

FAUSTUS. What art thou? the third.   305

WRATH. I am *Wrath*, I had neither father nor mother, I leapt
out of a lions mouth, when I was scarce half an houre olde,
and ever since I have runne up and downe the worlde, with
this case of rapiers wounding my selfe, when I had nobody
to fight withal: I was borne in hel, and looke to it, for some 310
of you shalbe my father.

FAUSTUS. What art thou? the fourth.

ENVY. I am *Envy*, begotten of a Chimney-sweeper, and an
Oyster wife, I cannot reade, and therefore wish al bookes
were burnt: I am leane with seeing others eate, O that there 315
would come a famine through all the worlde, that all might
die, and I live alone, then thou shouldst see how fatt I
would be: but must thou sit and I stand? come downe with a
vengeance.

FAUSTUS. Away envious rascall: what art thou? the fift.   320

GLUTTONY. Who I sir, I am *Gluttony*, my parents are al
dead, and the divel a peny they have left me, but a bare
pention, and that is 30. meales a day, and tenne beavers, a
small trifle to suffice nature, O I come of a royall parentage,
my grandfather was a gammon of bacon, my grandmother a 325
hogs head of Claret-wine: My godfathers were these, *Peter
Pickle-herring*, and *Martin Martlemas-biefe*, O but my god-
mother she was a jolly gentlewoman, and welbeloved in
every good towne and Citie, her name was mistresse
Margery March-beere: now *Faustus*, thou hast heard all my 330
progeny, wilt thou bid me to supper?

FAUSTUS. No, Ile see thee hanged, thou wilt eate up all my
victualls.

GLUTTONY. Then the divell choake thee.

FAUSTUS. Choake thy selfe glutton: what art thou? the sixt. 335

SLOTH. I am *Sloath*, I was begotten on a sunny banke, where
I have laine ever since, and you have done me great injury to
bring me from thence, let me be carried thither againe by
Gluttony and *Leachery*, Ile not speake an other worde for a
Kings raunsome. 340

FAUSTUS. What are you mistresse minkes? the seaventh and
last.

LECHERY. Who I sir? I am one that loves an inch of raw
Mutton better then an ell of fride stock fish, and the first
letter of my name beginnes with *leachery*. 345

LUCIFER. Away, to hel, to hel. *exeunt the* SINNES.
Now *Faustus*, how dost thou like this?

FAUSTUS. O this feedes my soule.

LUCIFER. Tut *Faustus*, in hel is al manner of delight.

FAUSTUS. O might I see hel, and returne againe, how happy 350
were I then?

LUCIFER. Thou shalt, I wil send for thee at midnight, in
meane time take this booke, peruse it throwly, and thou
shalt turne thy selfe into what shape thou wilt.

FAUSTUS. Great thankes mighty *Lucifer*, this wil I keepe as 355
chary as my life.

LUCIFER. Farewel *Faustus*, and thinke on the divel.

FAUSTUS. Farewel great *Lucifer*, come *Mephastophilis*.

exeunt omnes.

[Scene 6]

Enter ROBIN *the Ostler with a booke in his hand.*

ROBIN. O this is admirable! here I ha stolne one of doctor
Faustus conjuring books, and ifaith I meane to search some
circles for my owne use: now wil I make al the maidens in
our parish dance at my pleasure starke naked before me, and
so by that meanes I shal see more then ere I felt, or saw yet. 5

Scene 6 follows the papal banquet in A, where it is immediately followed by the theft of the
goblet (here scene 8).

Enter RAFE *calling* ROBIN.

RAFE. *Robin*, prethee come away, there a Gentleman tarries to
  have his horse, and he would have his things rubd and made
  cleane: he keepes such a chafing with my mistris about it,
  and she has sent me to looke thee out, prethee come away.

ROBIN. Keepe out, keep out, or else you are blowne up, you   10
  are dismembred *Rafe*, keepe out, for I am about a roaring
  peece of worke.

RAFE. Come, what doest thou with that same booke thou
  canst not reade?

ROBIN. Yes, my maister and mistris shall find that I can   15
  reade, he for his forehead, she for her private study, shee's
  borne to beare with me, or else my Art failes.

RAFE. Why *Robin* what booke is that?

ROBIN. What booke? why the most intollerable booke for
  conjuring that ere was invented by any brimstone divel.   20

RAFE. Canst thou conjure with it?

ROBIN. I can do al these things easily with it: first, I can make
  thee druncke with ipocrase at any taberne in Europe for
  nothing, thats one of my conjuring workes.

RAFE. Our maister Parson sayes thats nothing.   25

ROBIN. True *Rafe*, and more *Rafe*, if thou hast any mind to
  Nan Spit our kitchin maide, then turne her and wind hir to
  thy owne use, as often as thou wilt, and at midnight.

RAFE. O brave *Robin*, shall I have *Nan Spit*, and to mine
  owne use? On that condition Ile feede thy divel with horse-   30
  bread as long as he lives, of free cost.

ROBIN. No more sweete *Rafe*, letts goe and make cleane our
  bootes which lie foule upon our handes, and then to our
  conjuring in the divels name.   *exeunt*.

[Chorus 2]

Enter WAGNER *solus*.

WAGNER. Learned *Faustus*,
  To know the secrets of Astronomy,
  Graven in the booke of *Joves* hie firmament,

Did mount himselfe to scale *Olympus* top,
Being seated in a chariot burning bright,   5
Drawne by the strength of yoked dragons neckes,
He now is gone to proove Cosmography,
And as I guesse, wil first arive at *Rome*,
To see the Pope, and manner of his court,
And take some part of holy *Peters* feast,   10
That to this day is highly solemnizd.   *exit* WAGNER.

[Scene 7]

Enter FAUSTUS *and* MEPHASTOPHILUS.

FAUSTUS. Having now, my good *Mephastophilus*,
    Past with delight the stately towne of *Trier*,
    Invirond round with ayrie mountaine tops,
    With walles of flint, and deepe intrenched lakes,
    Not to be wonne by any conquering prince,   5
    From *Paris* next coasting the Realme of *France*,
    Wee sawe the river *Maine* fall into *Rhine*,
    Whose bankes are set with groves of fruitful vines.
    Then up to *Naples*, rich *Campania*,
    Whose buildings faire and gorgeous to the eye,   10
    The streetes straight forth, and pav'd with finest bricke,
    Quarters the towne in foure equivolence.
    There saw we learned *Maroes* golden tombe,
    The way he cut an *English* mile in length,
    Thorough a rocke of stone in one nights space.   15
    From thence to *Venice*, *Padua*, and the rest,
    In midst of which a sumptuous Temple stands,
    That threats the starres with her aspiring toppe.
    Thus hitherto hath *Faustus* spent his time,
    But tell me now, what resting place is this?   20
    Hast thou as erst I did commaund,
    Conducted me within the walles of *Rome*?
MEPHASTOPHILIS. *Faustus* I have, and because we wil not

6 yoked] *B*; yoky *A*

be unprovided, I have taken up his holinesse privy chamber
for our use.   25
FAUSTUS. I hope his holinesse will bid us welcome.
MEPHASTOPHILIS. Tut, tis no matter man, weele be bold
    with his good cheare,
And now my *Faustus*, that thou maist perceive
What *Rome* containeth to delight thee with,   30
Know that this Citie stands upon seven hilles
That underprops the groundworke of the same,
[Just through the midst runnes flowing *Tybers* streame,
With winding bankes that cut it in two parts;]
Over the which foure stately bridges leane,   35
That makes safe passage to each part of *Rome*.
Upon the bridge call'd *Ponto Angelo*,
Erected is a Castle passing strong,
Within whose walles such store of ordonance are,
And double Canons, fram'd of carved brasse,   40
As match the dayes within one compleate yeare,
Besides the gates and high piramides,
Which *Julius Caesar* brought from *Affrica*.
FAUSTUS. Now by the kingdomes of infernall rule,
Of *Styx*, *Acheron*, and the fiery lake   45
Of ever-burning *Phlegiton* I sweare,
That I do long to see the monuments
And scituation of bright splendant *Rome*,
Come therefore lets away.
MEPHASTOPHILIS. Nay *Faustus* stay, I know youd faine see
    the Pope   50
And take some part of holy *Peters* feast,
Where thou shalt see a troupe of bald-pate Friers,
Whose *summum bonum* is in belly-cheare.
FAUSTUS. Well, I am content, to compasse then some sport,
And by their folly make us merriment,   55
Then charme me that I may be invisible, to do what I please
unseene of any whilst I stay in *Rome*.
MEPHASTOPHILIS. So *Faustus*, now do what thou wilt, thou
    shalt not be discerned.

Sound a Sennet, enter the POPE *and the* CARDINALL
of LORRAINE *to the banket, with* FRIERS *attending.*

POPE. My Lord of *Lorraine*, wilt please you draw neare.   60
FAUSTUS. Fall too, and the divel choake you and you spare.
POPE. How now, whose that which spake? Friers looke about.
FRIAR. Heere's no body, if it like your Holynesse.
POPE. My Lord, here is a daintie dish was sent me from the
  Bishop of *Millaine*.   65
FAUSTUS. I thanke you sir.   *Snatch it.*
POPE. How now, whose that which snatcht the meate from
  me? will no man looke? My Lord, this dish was sent me
  from the Cardinall of *Florence*.
FAUSTUS. You say true, Ile hate.   [*Snatch againe.*]
POPE. What againe? my Lord Ile drinke to your grace.
FAUSTUS. Ile pledge your grace.   [*Snatch againe.*]
LORRAINE. My Lord, it may be some ghost newly crept out
  of Purgatory come to begge a pardon of your holinesse.
POPE. It may be so, Friers prepare a dirge to lay the fury of   75
  this ghost, once againe my Lord fall too.
                            The POPE *crosseth himselfe.*
FAUSTUS. What, are you crossing of your selfe?
  Well use that tricke no more, I would advise you.
                                            Crosse againe.
FAUSTUS. Well, theres the second time, aware the third, I
  give you faire warning.   80

      Crosse againe, and FAUSTUS *hits him a boxe of the eare
                    and they all runne away.*

FAUSTUS. Come on *Mephastophilis*, what shall we do?
MEPHASTOPHILIS. Nay I know not, we shalbe curst with
  bell, booke, and candle.
FAUSTUS. How? bell, booke, and candle, candle, booke, and
  bell,
  Forward and backward, to curse *Faustus* to hell.   85
  Anon you shal heare a hogge grunt, a calfe bleate, and an
  asse bray,
  Because it is S. *Peters* holy day.

      Enter all the FRIERS *to sing the Dirge.*

FRIAR. Come brethren, lets about our businesse with good
    devotion.   *Sing this.*
    Cursed be hee that stole away his holinesse meate from the
    table.
                          maledicat dominus.
    Cursed be hee that strooke his holinesse a blowe on the face.
                          maledicat dominus.   95
    Cursed be he that tooke Frier *Sandelo* a blow on the pate.
                          male, &c.
    Cursed be he that disturbeth our holy Dirge.
                          male, &c.
    Cursed be he that tooke away his holinesse wine.   100
                          maledicat dominus.
                   Et omnes sancti Amen

       Beate the FRIERS, *and fling fier-workes among*
                them, and so Exeunt.

[Scene 8]

Enter ROBIN *and* RAFE *with a silver Goblet.*

ROBIN. Come *Rafe*, did not I tell thee, we were for ever made
    by this doctor *Faustus* booke? *ecce signum*, heeres a simple
    purchase for horse-keepers, our horses shall eate no hay as
    long as this lasts.
                   Enter the VINTNER.
RAFE. But *Robin*, here comes the vintner.   5
ROBIN. Hush, Ile gul him supernaturally: Drawer, I hope al
    is payd, God be with you, come *Rafe*.
VINTNER. Soft sir, a word with you, I must yet have a goblet
    payde from you ere you goe.
ROBIN. I a goblet *Rafe*, I a goblet? I scorne you: and you are   10
    but a &c. I a goblet? search me.
VINTNER. I meane so sir with your favor.
ROBIN. How say you now?
VINTNER. I must say somewhat to your felow, you sir.
RAFE. Me sir, me sir, search your fill: now sir, you may be   15
    ashamed to burden honest men with a matter of truth.

VINTNER. Wel, tone of you hath this goblet about you.

ROBIN. You lie Drawer, tis afore me: sirra you, Ile teach ye to
impeach honest men: stand by, Ile scowre you for a goblet,
[*to* RAFE] stand aside you had best, I charge you in the   20
name of *Belzabub*: looke to the goblet *Rafe*.

VINTNER. What meane you sirra?

ROBIN. Ile tell you what I meane.   *He reades.*
Sanctobulorum Periphrasticon; nay Ile tickle you Vintner,
looke to the goblet *Rafe, Polypragmos Belseborams framanto*   25
pacostiphos Mephastophilis, &c.

> *Enter* MEPHASTOPHILIS: *sets squibs at their backes:*
> *they runne about.*

VINTNER. *O nomine Domine,* what meanst thou *Robin*? thou
hast no goblet.   [*exit* VINTNER.]

RAFE. *Peccatum peccatorum,* heeres thy goblet, good Vintner.

ROBIN. *Misericordia pro nobis,* what shal I doe? good divel   30
forgive me now, and Ile never rob thy Library more.

> *Enter to them* MEPH.

MEPHASTOPHILIS. Vanish vilaines, th'one like an Ape, an
other like a Beare, the third an Asse, for doing this enter-
prise.
Monarch of hel, under whose blacke survey   35
Great Potentates do kneele with awful feare,
Upon whose altars thousand soules do lie,
How am I vexed with these vilaines charmes?
From *Constantinople* am I hither come,
Onely for pleasure of these damned slaves.   40

ROBIN. How, from *Constantinople*? you have had a great journey, wil you take sixe pence in your purse to pay for your
supper, and be gone?

MEPHASTOPHILIS. Wel villaines, for your presumption, I
transforme thee into an Ape, and thee into a Dog, and so be   45
gone.   *exit.*

ROBIN. How, into an Ape? thats brave, Ile have fine sport
with the boyes, Ile get nuts and apples enow.

RAFE. And I must be a Dogge.

ROBIN. Ifaith thy head wil never be out of the potage pot.   50
                                            exeunt.

[Chorus 3]

Enter CHORUS.

When *Faustus* had with pleasure tane the view
Of rarest things, and royal courts of kings,
Hee stayde his course, and so returned home,
Where such as beare his absence, but with griefe,
I meane his friends and nearest companions,   5
Did gratulate his safetie with kinde words,
And in their conference of what befell,
Touching his journey through the world and ayre,
They put forth questions of Astrologie,
Which *Faustus* answerd with such learned skill,   10
As they admirde and wondred at his wit.
Now is his fame spread forth in every land,
Amongst the rest the Emperour is one,
Carolus the fift, at whose pallace now
Faustus is feasted mongst his noblemen.   15
What there he did in triall of his art,
I leave untold, your eyes shall see performd.   *Exit.*

[Scene 9]

Enter EMPEROUR, FAUSTUS, [MEPHASTOPHILIS,]
and a KNIGHT, *with Attendants.*

EMPEROR. Maister doctor *Faustus*, I have heard strange
report of thy knowledge in the blacke Arte, how that none in
my Empire, nor in the whole world can compare with thee,
for the rare effects of Magicke: they say thou hast a familiar
spirit, by whome thou canst accomplish what thou list, this   5
therefore is my request that thou let me see some proofe of
thy skil, that mine eies may be witnesses to confirme what
mine eares have heard reported, and here I sweare to thee,

Chorus 3: *in the A text this Chorus precedes the combined clownage scenes here printed as scenes 6 and 8.*

by the honor of mine Imperial crowne, that what ever thou
doest, thou shalt be in no wayes prejudiced or indamaged.   10

KNIGHT. Ifaith he lookes much like a conjurer.   *aside*.

FAUSTUS. My gratious Soveraigne, though I must confesse
my selfe farre inferior to the report men have published,
and nothing answerable to the honor of your Imperial
majesty, yet for that love and duety bindes me thereunto, I   15
am content to do whatsoever your majesty shall command
me.

EMPEROR. Then doctor *Faustus*, marke what I shall say, As I
was sometime solitary set, within my Closet, sundry
thoughts arose, about the honour of mine auncestors, howe   20
they had wonne by prowesse such exploits, gote such riches,
subdued so many kingdomes, as we that do succeede, or
they that shal hereafter possesse our throne, shal (I feare
me) never attaine to that degree of high renowne and great
authoritie, amongest which kings is *Alexander* the great,   25
chiefe spectacle of the worldes preheminence.
The bright shining of whose glorious actes
Lightens the world with his reflecting beames,
As when I heare but motion made of him,
It grieves my soule I never saw the man: 30
If therefore thou, by cunning of thine Art,
Canst raise this man from hollow vaults below,
Where lies intombde this famous Conquerour,
And bring with him his beauteous Paramour,
Both in their right shapes, gesture, and attire   35
They usde to weare during their time of life,
Thou shalt both satisfie my just desire,
And give me cause to praise thee whilst I live.

FAUSTUS. My gratious Lord, I am ready to accomplish your
request, so farre forth as by art and power of my spirit I am 40
able to performe.

KNIGHT. Ifaith thats just nothing at all.   *aside*.

FAUSTUS. But if it like your Grace, it is not in my abilitie to
present before your eyes, the true substantiall bodies of
those two deceased princes which long since are consumed   45
to dust.

KNIGHT. I mary master doctor, now theres a signe of grace in
you, when you will confesse the trueth.   *aside*.

FAUSTUS. But such spirites as can lively resemble *Alexander*
and his Paramour, shal appeare before your Grace, in that   50
manner that they best liv'd in, in their most florishing
estate, which I doubt not shal sufficiently content your
Imperiall majesty.

EMPEROR. Go to maister Doctor, let me see them presently.

KNIGHT. Do you heare maister Doctor? you bring *Alexander*   55
and his paramour before the emperor?

FAUSTUS. How then sir?

KNIGHT. Ifaith thats as true as *Diana* turnd me to a stag.

FAUSTUS. No sir but when *Acteon* died, he left the hornes for
you: *Mephastophilis* be gone.   60

exit MEPH.

KNIGHT. Nay, and you go to conjuring, Ile be gone.

exit KN:

FAUSTUS. Ile meete with you anone for interrupting me so:
heere they are my gratious Lord.

Enter MEPH: *with Alexander and his paramour.*

EMPEROR. Maister Doctor, I heard this Lady while she liv'd
had a wart or moale in her necke, how shal I know whether   65
it be so or no?

FAUSTUS. Your highnes may boldly go and see.

exit Alex: [*and his paramour*].

EMPEROR. Sure these are no spirites, but the true substantiall bodies of those two deceased princes.

FAUSTUS. Wilt please your highnes now to send for the   70
knight that was so pleasant with me here of late?

EMPEROR. One of you call him foorth.

Enter the KNIGHT *with a paire of hornes on his head.*

EMPEROR. How now sir Knight? why I had thought thou
hadst beene a batcheler, but now I see thou hast a wife, that
not only gives thee hornes, but makes thee weare them, feele 75
on thy head.

KNIGHT. Thou damned wretch, and execrable dogge,
Bred in the concave of some monstrous rocke:
How darst thou thus abuse a Gentleman?
Vilaine I say, undo what thou hast done.   80

FAUSTUS. O not so fast sir, theres no haste but good, are you remembred how you crossed me in my conference with the emperour? I thinke I have met with you for it.

EMPEROR. Good Maister Doctor, at my intreaty release him, he hath done penance sufficient.   85

FAUSTUS. My Gratious Lord, not so much for the injury hee offred me heere in your presence, as to delight you with some mirth, hath *Faustus* worthily requited this injurious knight, which being all I desire, I am content to release him of his hornes: and sir knight, hereafter speake well of   90 Scholers: *Mephastophilis*, transforme him strait. Now my good Lord having done my duety, I humbly take my leave.

EMPEROR. Farewel maister Doctor, yet ere you goe, expect from me a bounteous reward.   *exit* EMPEROUR.

FAUSTUS. Now *Mephastophilis*, the restlesse course   95
That time doth runne with calme and silent foote,
Shortning my dayes and thred of vitall life,
Calls for the payment of my latest yeares,
Therefore sweet *Mephastophilis*, let us make haste to
Wertenberge.   100

MEPHASTOPHILIS. What, wil you goe on horse backe, or on foote?

FAUSTUS. Nay, til I am past this faire and pleasant greene, ile walke on foote.

[Scene 10]

Enter [to them] a HORSE-COURSER.

HORSE-COURSER. I have beene al this day seeking one maister *Fustian*: masse see where he is, God save you maister doctor.

FAUSTUS. What horse-courser, you are wel met.

HORSE-COURSER. Do you heare sir? I have brought you   5
forty dollers for your horse.

FAUSTUS. I cannot sel him so: if thou likst him for fifty, take him.

HORSE-COURSER. Alas sir, I have no more, I pray you speake for me.   10

MEPHASTOPHILIS. I pray you let him have him, he is an honest felow, and he has a great charge, neither wife nor childe.

FAUSTUS. Wel, come give me your money, my boy wil deliver him to you: but I must tel you one thing before you have him, ride him not into the water at any hand. 15

HORSE-COURSER. Why sir, wil he not drinke of all waters?

FAUSTUS. O yes, he wil drinke of al waters, but ride him not into the water, ride him over hedge or ditch, or where thou wilt, but not into the water. 20

HORSE-COURSER. Wel sir, Now am I made man for ever, Ile not leave my horse for fortie: if he had but the qualitie of hey ding, ding, hey, ding, ding, Ide make a brave living on him; hee has a buttocke as slicke as an Ele: wel god buy sir, your boy wil deliver him me: but hark ye sir, if my horse be 25 sick, or ill at ease, if I bring his water to you youle tel me what it is? *Exit* HORSE-COURSER.

FAUSTUS. Away you villaine: what, dost thinke I am a horse-doctor?
What art thou *Faustus* but a man condemned to die? 30
Thy fatall time doth drawe to finall ende,
Dispaire doth drive distrust unto my thoughts,
Confound these passions with a quiet sleepe:
Tush, *Christ* did call the thiefe vpon the Crosse,
Then rest thee *Faustus* quiet in conceit. 35
Sleepe in his chaire.

Enter HORSECOURSER *all wet, crying.*

HORSE-COURSER. Alas, alas, Doctor *Fustian* quoth a, mas Doctor *Lopus* was never such a Doctor, has given me a purgation, has purg'd me of fortie Dollers, I shall never see them more: but yet like an asse as I was, I would not be ruled by him, for he bade me I should ride him into no 40 water; now, I thinking my horse had had some rare qualitie that he would not have had me knowne of, I like a ventrous youth, rid him into the deepe pond at the townes ende, I was no sooner in the middle of the pond, but my horse vanisht away, and I sat upon a bottle of hey, never so neare 45 drowning in my life: but Ile seeke out my Doctor, and have my fortie dollers againe, or Ile make it the dearest horse: O

yonder is his snipper snapper, do you heare? you, hey,
passe, where's your maister?

MEPHASTOPHILIS. Why sir, what would you? you cannot   50
speake with him.

HORSE-COURSER. But I wil speake with him.

MEPHASTOPHILIS. Why hee's fast asleepe, come some
other time.

HORSE-COURSER. Ile speake with him now, or Ile breake   55
his glasse-windowes about his eares.

MEPHASTOPHILIS. I tell thee he has not slept this eight
nights.

HORSE-COURSER. And he have not slept this eight weekes
Ile speake with him.   60

MEPHASTOPHILIS. See where he is fast asleepe.

HORSE-COURSER. I, this is he, God save ye maister doctor,
maister doctor, maister doctor *Fustian*, fortie dollers, fortie
dollers for a bottle of hey.

MEPHASTOPHILIS. Why, thou seest he heares thee not.   65

HORSE-COURSER. So, ho, ho: so, ho, ho.   *Hallow in his eare.*
No, will you not wake? Ile make you wake ere I goe.
                    Pull him by the legge, and pull it away.
Alas, I am undone, what shall I do?

FAUSTUS. O my legge, my legge, helpe *Mephastophilis*, call
the Officers, my legge, my legge.   70

MEPHASTOPHILIS. Come villaine to the Constable.

HORSE-COURSER. O Lord sir, let me goe, and Ile give you
fortie dollers more.

MEPHASTOPHILIS. Where be they?

HORSE-COURSER. I have none about me, come to my Oas-   75
trie and Ile give them you.

MEPHASTOPHILIS. Be gone quickly.
                         HORSECOURSER *runnes away.*

FAUSTUS. What is he gone? farwel he, *Faustus* has his legge
againe, and the Horsecourser I take it, a bottle of hey for his
labour; wel, this tricke shal cost him fortie dollers more.   80

                    Enter WAGNER.

How now *Wagner*, what's the newes with thee?

WAGNER. Sir, the Duke of *Vanholt* doth earnestly entreate
your company.

FAUSTUS. The Duke of *Vanholt*! an honourable gentleman,
to whom I must be no niggard of my cunning, come   85
Mephastophilis, let's away to him.   *exeunt.*

[Scene 11]

[FAUSTUS *and* MEPHASTOPHILIS *return to the stage.*]
Enter to them the DUKE, *and the* DUTCHES,
the DUKE *speakes.*

DUKE. Beleeve me maister Doctor, this merriment hath much
pleased me.

FAUSTUS. My gratious Lord, I am glad it contents you so
wel: but it may be Madame, you take no delight in this, I
have heard that great bellied women do long for some dain-   5
ties or other, what is it Madame? tell me, and you shal have
it.

DUCHESS. Thankes, good maister doctor, And for I see your
curteous intent to pleasure me, I wil not hide from you the
thing my heart desires, and were it nowe summer, as it is   10
January, and the dead time of the winter, I would desire no
better meate then a dish of ripe grapes.

FAUSTUS. Alas Madame, thats nothing, *Mephastophilis*, be gone:
                                    exit MEPH.

were it a greater thing then this, so it would content you,
you should have it,   15

Enter MEPHASTO: *with the grapes.*

here they be madam, wilt please you taste on them.

DUKE. Beleeve me master Doctor, this makes me wonder
above the rest, that being in the dead time of winter, and
in the month of January, how you shuld come by these
grapes.   20

FAUSTUS. If it like your grace, the yeere is divided into twoo
circles over the whole worlde, that when it is heere winter
with us, in the contrary circle it is summer with them, as in
India, *Saba*, and farther countries in the East, and by means

of a swift spirit that I have, I had them brought hither, as ye   25
see, how do you like them Madame, be they good?

DUCHESS. Beleeve me Maister doctor, they be the best
grapes that ere I tasted in my life before.

FAUSTUS. I am glad they content you so Madam.

DUKE. Come Madame, let us in, where you must wel reward   30
this learned man for the great kindnes he hath shewd to
you.

DUCHESS. And so I wil my Lord, and whilst I live, rest
beholding for this curtesie.

FAUSTUS. I humbly thanke your Grace.   35

DUKE. Come maister Doctor follow us, and receive your
reward.   *exeunt.*

[Chorus 4]

Enter WAGNER *solus.*

WAGNER. I thinke my maister meanes to die shortly,
    For he hath given to me al his goodes,
    And yet me thinkes, if that death were neere,
    He would not banquet, and carowse, and swill
    Amongst the Students, as even now he doth,   5
    Who are at supper with such belly-cheere,
    As *Wagner* nere beheld in all his life.
    See where they come: belike the feast is ended.   [*Exit.*]

[Scene 12]

Enter FAUSTUS [*and* MEPHASTOPHILIS]
with two or three SCHOLLERS.

1 SCHOLAR. Maister Doctor *Faustus*, since our conference
about faire Ladies, which was the beutifulst in all the world,
we have determined with our selves, that *Helen* of *Greece*
was the admirablest Lady that ever lived: therefore master

Doctor, if you wil do us that favor, as to let us see that   5
peerelesse Dame of *Greece*, whome al the world admires for
majesty, wee should thinke our selves much beholding unto
you.

FAUSTUS. Gentlemen, for that I know your friendship is
unfained, and *Faustus* custome is not to denie the just re-   10
quests of those that wish him well, you shall behold that
pearelesse dame of *Greece*, no otherwaies for pompe and
majestie, then when sir *Paris* crost the seas with her, and
brought the spoiles to rich *Dardania*. Be silent then, for
danger is in words.   15

    Musicke sounds, and Helen passeth over the Stage.

2 SCHOLAR. Too simple is my wit to tell her praise,
  Whom all the world admires for majestie.

3 SCHOLAR. No marvel tho the angry *Greekes* pursude
  With tenne yeares warre the rape of such a queene,
  Whose heavenly beauty passeth all compare.   20

1 SCHOLAR. Since we have seene the pride of natures
workes,
  And onely Paragon of excellence,

    Enter an OLD MAN.

Let us depart, and for this glorious deed
Happy and blest be *Faustus* evermore.

FAUSTUS. Gentlemen farwel, the same I wish to you.   25

    Exeunt SCHOLLERS.

OLD MAN. Ah Doctor *Faustus*, that I might prevaile,
  To guide thy steps unto the way of life,
  By which sweete path thou maist attaine the gole
  That shall conduct thee to celestial rest.
  Breake heart, drop bloud, and mingle it with teares,   30
  Teares falling from repentant heavinesse
  Of thy most vilde and loathsome filthinesse,
  The stench whereof corrupts the inward soule
  With such flagitious crimes of hainous sinnes,
  As no commiseration may expel,   35
  But mercie *Faustus* of thy Saviour sweete,
  Whose bloud alone must wash away thy guilt.

FAUSTUS. Where art thou *Faustus*? wretch what hast thou
done?

Damnd art thou *Faustus*, damnd, dispaire and die.
Hell calls for right, and with a roaring voyce   40
Sayes, *Faustus* come, thine houre is come,
                                    MEPHA. *gives him a dagger.*
And *Faustus* will come to do thee right.
OLD MAN. Ah stay good *Faustus*, stay thy desperate steps,
    I see an Angell hovers ore thy head,
    And with a violl full of precious grace,   45
    Offers to powre the same into thy soule,
    Then call for mercie and avoyd dispaire.
FAUSTUS. Ah my sweete friende, I feele thy words
    To comfort my distressed soule,
    Leave me a while to ponder on my sinnes.   50
OLD MAN. I goe sweete *Faustus*, but with heavy cheare,
    Fearing the ruine of thy hopelesse soule.
FAUSTUS. Accursed *Faustus*, where is mercie now?
    I do repent, and yet I do dispaire:
    Hell strives with grace for conquest in my breast,   55
    What shal I do to shun the snares of death?
MEPHASTOPHILIS. Thou traitor *Faustus*, I arrest thy soule
    For disobedience to my soveraigne Lord,
    Revolt, or Ile in peece-meale teare thy flesh.
FAUSTUS. Sweete *Mephastophilis*, intreate thy Lord   60
    To pardon my unjust presumption,
    And with my blood againe I wil confirme
    My former vow I made to *Lucifer*.
MEPHASTOPHILIS. Do it then quickely, with unfained
    heart,
    Lest greater danger do attend thy drift.   65
FAUSTUS. Torment sweete friend, that base and crooked age,
    That durst disswade me from thy *Lucifer*,
    With greatest torments that our hel affoords.
MEPHASTOPHILIS. His faith is great, I cannot touch his soule,
    But what I may afflict his body with,   70
    I wil attempt, which is but little worth.
FAUSTUS. One thing, good servant, let me crave of thee
    To glut the longing of my hearts desire,
    That I might have unto my paramour,
    That heavenly *Helen* which I saw of late,   75
    Whose sweete imbracings may extinguish cleane

These thoughts that do disswade me from my vow,
And keepe mine oath I made to *Lucifer*.
MEPHASTOPHILIS. *Faustus*, this, or what else thou shalt
    desire,
Shalbe performde in twinckling of an eie.   80

Enter Helen.

FAUSTUS. Was this the face that lancht a thousand shippes?
And burnt the toplesse Towres of *Ilium*?
Sweete *Helen*, make me immortall with a kisse:
Her lips suckes forth my soule, see where it flies:
Come *Helen*, come give mee my soule againe.   85
Here wil I dwel, for heaven be in these lips,
And all is drosse that is not *Helena*:

Enter OLD MAN.

I wil be *Paris*, and for love of thee,
Insteede of *Troy* shal *Wertenberge* be sackt,
And I wil combate with weake *Menelaus*,   90
And weare thy colours on my plumed Crest:
Yea I wil wound *Achillis* in the heele,
And then returne to *Helen* for a kisse.
O thou art fairer then the evening aire,
Clad in the beauty of a thousand starres,   95
Brighter art thou then flaming *Jupiter*,
When he appeard to haplesse *Semele*,
More lovely then the monarke of the skie
In wanton *Arethusaes* azurde armes,
And none but thou shalt be my paramour.   *Exeunt.*
OLD MAN. Accursed *Faustus*, miserable man,
That from thy soule excludst the grace of heaven,
And fliest the throne of his tribunall seate,

Enter the Divelles.

Sathan begins to sift me with his pride,
As in this furnace God shal try my faith,   105
My faith, vile hel, shal triumph over thee,
Ambitious fiends, see how the heavens smiles
At your repulse, and laughs your state to scorne,
Hence hel, for hence I flie unto my God.   *Exeunt.*

[Scene 13]

Enter FAUSTUS *with the* SCHOLLERS.

FAUSTUS. Ah Gentlemen!

1 SCHOLAR. What ailes *Faustus*?

FAUSTUS. Ah my sweete chamber-fellow! had I lived with
thee, then had I lived stil, but now I die eternally: looke,
comes he not? comes he not?   5

2 SCHOLAR. What meanes *Faustus*?

3 SCHOLAR. Belike he is growne into some sicknesse, by
being over solitary.

1 SCHOLAR. If it be so, weele have Physitians to cure him, tis
but a surfett, never feare man.   10

FAUSTUS. A surfett of deadly sinne that hath damnd both
body and soule.

2 SCHOLAR. Yet *Faustus* looke up to heaven, remember
Gods mercies are infinite.

FAUSTUS. But *Faustus* offence can nere be pardoned,   15
The Serpent that tempted *Eve* may be sav'd,
But not *Faustus*: Ah Gentlemen, heare me with patience,
and tremble not at my speeches, though my heart pants and
quivers to remember that I have beene a student here these
thirty yeeres, O would I had never seene *Wertenberge*, never 20
read booke: and what wonders I have done, al *Germany* can
witnes, yea all the world, for which *Faustus* hath lost both
Germany, and the world, yea heaven it selfe, heaven the
seate of God, the throne of the blessed, the kingdome of joy,
and must remaine in hel for ever, hel, ah hel for ever, sweete 25
friends, what shall become of *Faustus*, being in hel for
ever?

3 SCHOLAR. Yet *Faustus* call on God.

FAUSTUS. On God whome *Faustus* hath abjurde, on God
whome *Faustus* hath blasphemed, ah my God, I woulde   30
weepe, but the divel drawes in my teares, gush foorth bloud,
insteade of teares, yea life and soule, Oh he stayes my tong,
I would lift up my hands, but see, they hold them, they hold
them.

ALL. Who *Faustus*?   35

FAUSTUS. *Lucifer* and *Mephastophilis*. Ah Gentlemen! I gave
them my soule for my cunning.

ALL. God forbid.

FAUSTUS. God forbade it indeede, but *Faustus* hath done it:
for the vaine pleasure of foure and twentie yeares, hath   40
Faustus lost eternall joy and felicitie, I writ them a bill with
mine owne bloud, the date is expired, the time wil come,
and he wil fetch mee.

1 SCHOLAR. Why did not *Faustus* tel us of this before, that
Divines might have prayed for thee?   45

FAUSTUS. Oft have I thought to have done so, but the divell
threatned to teare mee in peeces, if I namde God, to fetch
both body and soule, if I once gave eare to divinitie: and
now tis too late: Gentlemen away, lest you perish with me.

2 SCHOLAR. O what shal we do to save *Faustus*?   50

3 SCHOLAR. God wil strengthen me, I wil stay with *Faustus*.

1 SCHOLAR. Tempt not God, sweete friend, but let us into
the next roome, and there pray for him.

FAUSTUS. I pray for me, pray for me, and what noyse soever
yee heare, come not unto me, for nothing can rescue me.   55

2 SCHOLAR. Pray thou, and we wil pray that God may have
mercy upon thee.

FAUSTUS. Gentlemen farewel, if I live til morning, Ile visite
you: if not, *Faustus* is gone to hel.

ALL. *Faustus*, farewel.   *Exeunt* SCH.

The clocke strikes eleaven.

FAUSTUS. Ah *Faustus*,
Now hast thou but one bare hower to live,
And then thou must be damnd perpetually:
Stand stil you ever mooving spheres of heaven,
That time may cease, and midnight never come: 65
Faire Natures eie, rise, rise againe, and make
Perpetuall day, or let this houre be but a yeere,
A moneth, a weeke, a naturall day,
That *Faustus* may repent and save his soule,
O lente lente curite noctis equi: 70
The starres moove stil, time runs, the clocke wil strike,
The divel wil come, and *Faustus* must be damnd.

40 for the vaine] *B*; ~ ∧ ~ *A*   50 to save *Faustus*] *B*; ~ ∧ ~ *A*

O Ile leape up to my God: who pulles me downe?
See see where *Christs* blood streames in the firmament,
One drop would save my soule, halfe a drop, ah my *Christ*,   75
Ah rend not my heart for naming of my *Christ*,
Yet wil I call on him, oh spare me *Lucifer*!
Where is it now? tis gone:
And see where God stretcheth out his arme,
And bends his irefull browes: 80
Mountaines and hilles, come come, and fall on me,
And hide me from the heavy wrath of God.
No no, then wil I headlong runne into the earth:
Earth gape, O no, it wil not harbour me:
You starres that raignd at my nativitie,   85
Whose influence hath alotted death and hel,
Now draw up *Faustus* like a foggy mist,
Into the intrailes of yon labring cloude,
That when you vomite foorth into the ayre,
My limbes may issue from your smoaky mouthes,   90
So that my soule may but ascend to heaven:
Ah, halfe the houre is past: *The watch strikes.*
Twil all be past anone:
Oh God, if thou wilt not have mercy on my soule,
Yet for *Christs* sake, whose bloud hath ransomd me,   95
Impose some end to my incessant paine,
Let *Faustus* live in hel a thousand yeeres,
A hundred thousand, and at last be sav'd.
O no end is limited to damned soules,
Why wert thou not a creature wanting soule?   100
Or, why is this immortall that thou hast?
Ah *Pythagoras metem su cossis* were that true,
This soule should flie from me, and I be changde
Unto some brutish beast: al beasts are happy, for when they
die,
Their soules are soone dissolvd in elements,   105
But mine must live still to be plagde in hel:
Curst be the parents that ingendred me:
No *Faustus*, curse thy selfe, curse *Lucifer*,
That hath deprivde thee of the joyes of heaven:
                            The clocke striketh twelve.
O it strikes, it strikes, now body turne to ayre,   110

Or *Lucifer* wil beare thee quicke to hel.

                       Thunder and lightning.

Oh soule, be changde into little water drops,
And fal into the Ocean, nere be found:
My God, my God, looke not so fierce on me: *Enter divels.*
Adders, and Serpents, let me breathe a while: 115
Ugly hell gape not, come not *Lucifer*,
Ile burne my bookes, ah *Mephastophilis.*   *exeunt with him.*

[Epilogue]

Enter CHORUS.

Cut is the branch that might have growne ful straight,
And burned is *Apolloes* Laurel bough,
That sometime grew within this learned man:
Faustus is gone, regard his hellish fall,
Whose fiendful fortune may exhort the wise,   5
Onely to wonder at unlawful things,
Whose deepeness doth intise such forward wits,
To practise more than heavenly power permits.

                                  [Exit.]

      Terminat hora diem, Terminat Author opus.

ACCIDENTAL EMENDATIONS

PROLOGUE

2 *Carthaginians*] Carthaginians   19 Theologie] *Theologie*

SCENE 1

6 *Analutikes*] *Anulatikes*   21 Whereby] whereby   35 Who] who
37 When] when   50 heavenly.] ~ ∧   65 *Germaine*] Germaine   *Valdes*]
Valde   *Cornelius*] *Corneliu*   69 Then] Thn   112 Consis sylogismes]
Consissylogismes   113 *Germaine*] Germaine   121 *Indian*] Indian   *Spanish*]
Spanish   126 *Lapland*] Lapland   130 dragge] dregge   143 *Delphian*]
Dolphian

SCENE 3

12 starres,] ~ .   13 rise.] ~ ,   17 *princeps,*] ~ ∧   18 *Belsibub*] ~ ,
46 *per accident*] per accident   48 *Christ*] Christ   55 principle,] ~ ∧
69 And] and   82 Which] which   91 foure and twentie] 24.   106 Ocean]
Ocean

SCENE 4

14 Wel] wel   18 How] how   31 Wel] wel   33 *french*] french (*also line 34*)
35 *english*] english   52 What] what   73 *Dutch*] Dutch

SCENE 5

1 *Faustus*] Faustus (*also at lines 6, 9, 15, 20, 21, 25, 31, 33, 34, 45, 59, 67, 69, 70, 75, 84,
87, 93*)   3 What] what   5 *Belsabub*] Belsabub (*also at line 12*)   7 Why]
why   12 Wherein] wherein   23 *Emden*] Emden   24 When] when
29SD *Enter*] enter   62 My] my (*lines 61 and 62 printed as prose in A*)
83 *Mephastophilis*] Mephastophilis (*also at lines 89, 215, 250*)   110 foure and
twentie] 24.   117 *Faustus*] Faustus (*also at lines 132, 136, 139, 152, 154, 186,194, 199,
203, 257, 263, 266, 271, 277, 281, 289, 290, 347, 349, 357*)   186 Why] why
194 repent, yet God] repent yet, God   196 Who] who   216 Astrologie]
Astrologie   223 termine] terminine   236 *Mercury*] Mercury
266 *Christ*] Christ (*also at lines 267, 273*)   272 We] we   292 *Pride*] Pride   312 What]
what   321 Who] who   326 *Peter Pickle-herring*] Peter Pickle-herring   327 *Martin
Martlemas-biefe*] Martin Martlemas-biefe   330 *Margery March-beere*] Margery
March-beere   336 *Sloath*] sloath   339 *Gluttony.*] Gluttony   *Leachery*]
Leachery   345 *leachery*] leachery   346 LUCIFER.] *The speech prefix has been moved
from line 347*   355 *Lucifer*] Lucifer

SCENE 6

2 *Faustus*] Faustus

CHORUS 2

0SD *Enter*] enter   1 *Faustus*] Faustus   2 Astronomy] *Astronomy*
7 Cosmography] *Cosmography*

SCENE 7

0SD *Enter*] enter   1 *Mephastophilus*] Mephastophilus   6 *France*] France
14 *English*] English   19 *Faustus*] Faustus (*also at lines 23, 29, 50, 58*)
26 holinesse] holiuesse (*turned n*)   57 *Rome*] Rome   59SD *Sennet*] Sonnet
69 *Florence*] Florence   81 *Mephastophilis*] Mephastophilis   87 Because]
because (*lines 86 and 87 printed as prose in A*)

SCENE 8
   2 *Faustus*] Faustus   4SD *Enter*] enter   21 *Belzabub*] Belzabub
22 What] what   44 Wel] wel

CHORUS 3
   1 *Faustus*] Faustus (*also at line 15*)

SCENE 9
   1 *Faustus*] Faustus (*also at line 18*)   33 Where] where   70 Wilt] wilt
95 *Mephastophilis*] Mephastophilis (*also at line 99*)   96 That] that (*lines 95 and 96 printed as prose in A*)   101 What] what

SCENE 10
   0SD *Enter*] enter   2 *Fustian*] Fustian (*also at lines 36, 63*) 17 Why] why
30 What] what (*lines 29 and 30 printed as prose in A*) *Faustus*] Faustus (*also at lines 35, 78*)
34 *Christ*] Christ   50 Why] why   68 do?] ~ :

SCENE 11
   15 it.] ~ ∧   15SD *Enter*] enter   33 rest] Rest (*new verse line in A*)

CHORUS 4
   0SD *Enter*] enter   6 Who] who

SCENE 12
   10 *Faustus*] Faustus (*also at lines 24, 26, 36, 38, 39, 41, 42, 43, 51, 53, 57*) denie] deuie
(*turned n*)   18 *Greekes*] Greekes   52 Fearing] fearing   81SD *Enter*] enter
(*and line 87*)   88 *Paris*] Pacis   97 When] when   104 *Sathan*] Sathan

SCENE 13
   2 What] what   2 *Faustus*] Faustus (*and throughout this scene*)   6 What]
what   14 Gods] gods   40 foure and twentie] 24.   44 Why] why
74 *Christs*] Christs (*and at line 95*)   75 *Christ*] Christ (*and at line 76*)
86 Whose] whose   113 Ocean] *Ocean*

EPILOGUE
   7 Whose] whose

COMMENTARY

Title-page

The printer's device on the title-page is identified as number 142 in McKerrow's *Printers' and Publishers' Devices*, where it is described as 'A boy with wings upon his right arm and with his left hand holding, or fastened to, a weight'. The emblem signifies talent frustrated by poverty. It was not unique to *Dr Faustus*: Simmes, the printer, had used it on several books, including the 1597 quarto of Shakespeare's *Richard II*.

Dramatis Personae

No list of *Dramatis Personae* is available before the edition of 1633; and the 1633 list is inaccurate. I have therefore supplied a list of characters in the A text.

Prologue

OSD CHORUS *OED* cites *Gorboduc* (1561) for the earliest use of this classical device for narrating the *faits d'avant scène*, linking the dramatic episodes, and commenting on their significance. The *Gorboduc* Chorus, in true Attic tradition, was composed of 'foure auncient and sage men of Brittaine'; and it seems to have been Marlowe who first used a single character (later identified with Wagner) to perform this role and fulfil the function of the 'Doctor', or presenter, of the morality plays. It was F. S. Boas who introduced the heading 'Prologue' into his edition of the play (1932), thereby insisting on the identification of the function of this choric figure with the one in Shakespeare's *Henry V* who pleads for the audience's entertainment of him:

> Admit me Chorus to this history:
> Who, Prologue like, your humble patience pray,
> Gently to hear, kindly to judge, our play. (Prologue, 32–4)

1–6 Not . . . verse] The references are unclear: if other works by Marlowe are intended, then the 'dalliance of love' could be that of *Dido Queene of Carthage* and the 'prowd audacious deedes' would be the conquests of *Tamburlaine the Great*. But Marlowe makes no mention anywhere else of Hannibal's victory at Lake Thrasymenus in 217 BC when the Romans suffered a spectacular defeat by the Carthaginians. The Roman god of war must have allied himself (*OED mate* $v^1$3) with the enemy on this occasion.

6 our Muse] i.e. our poet (not one of the nine Muses of the Greeks). Both Shakespeare and Milton have similar usages:

> So is it not with me as with that Muse
> Stirr'd by a painted beauty to his verse. (Sonnet XXI)

and

> So may some gentle Muse
> With lucky words favour my destined urn,
> And as he passes turn.   (*Lycidas*, lines 19–21)

6 vaunt] B's correction of A's 'daunt' is supported by *OED*, where *The Faerie Queene* is adduced to illustrate *vaunt* 4, 'to display proudly':

> What shape, what shield, what armes, what steed, what stel,
> And what so else his person most may vaunt.   (III. ii. 16)

7–8 performe, The forme] The rhetorical scheme of *polyptoton* is described by Peacham (*The Garden of Eloquence* (1577), p. 55) as 'A figure which of the word going before deriveth the word following . . . To delight the ear by the derived sound and to move the mind with a consideration of the high affinity and concord of the matter'. Cf. lines 16–17.

9 we appeale our plaude] The expression was apparently unfamiliar to the editor of the B text, who emended this line to read 'And now to patient judgements we appeale.' *Dr Faustus* is quoted as the earliest of *OED*'s examples of *plaud* = applause.

11–27 Now . . . blisse] Cf. Appendix A, ch. 1.

12 *Rhodes*] Stadtroda (near Jena, south-east of Weimar) is in East Germany.

13 *Wertenberg*] Wittenberg, Hamlet's university and Luther's, was the home of scepticism. But in all outward appearances Dr Faustus's *alma mater* is Marlowe's own Cambridge.

14 whereas] Where (*OED* 1).

15 soone] B's emendation to 'much' neglects the source's emphasis on the precociousness of the young Faustus.

16 The . . . grac't] The omission of this line in the B text suggests that B's editor, like Boas, found it 'obscure' and suspicious because of its anticipation of 'grac't' in the next line. But the two words combine into a form of *polyptoton*, one of Marlowe's favourite rhetorical devices (cf. lines 7–8). Scholarship was adorned (*OED grace* 4) by Faustus, just as he was honoured (*OED grace* 5) by the conferment of the doctor's degree.

Scholerisme] This term for scholarship, the 'learning of the schools', was often used disparagingly (like the adjective 'academic'). *OED* quotes a reference of 1611 to 'a miserable kinde of Schollerisme'.

17 grac't . . . name] Marlowe is thinking in familiar terms of the official 'grace' which permitted a candidate to proceed to his degree at the University of Cambridge. Marlowe's own name was entered in the Grace Book in 1584 and 1587.

18 disputes] The intransitive use of *dispute* is sense 1 of the verb in *OED*, where it is illustrated by a quotation from Chaucer's *Boethius*: 'The porche . . . of the toune of athenis ther as philosophres hadde hir congregacioun to dispoyten'. B attempts to simplify with its emendation: 'and sweetly can dispute'.

20 cunning] In the Authorized Version of the Bible (1613), the Psalmist vows 'If I forget thee, O Jerusalem, let my right hand forget her cunning' (Ps. 137: 5). At much the same date, Francis Bacon wrote in his essay 'Of Cunning' that 'we take cunning for a sinister and crooked wisdom'. The ambivalence of the word seems to have been appreciated by Marlowe.

selfe conceit] *OED conceit* 5b: 'Pride in oneself, or one's qualities'.

21 his waxen wings] Icarus, although counselled by his father 'to order well his flight' when using the wings that Daedalus had invented, ignored all warnings and

Of fond desire to flie to Heaven, above his boundes he stide.
And there the nereness of the Sunne which burnd more hote aloft,
Did make the Wax (with which his wings were glewed) lithe and soft.

Ovid tells the story in *Metamorphoses* (VIII. 264–313), and George Sandys, in his translation of the Latin (1632), commented on its significance:

This fable applauds the golden Meane, and flight of virtue betweene the two extreames. *Icarus* falls in aspiring. Yet more commendable than those, who creepe on the earth like contemptible wormes, such the other extreame: whereas this hath something of magnanimity, and mounts like the bird of *Jove* to his kindred Heaven. (George Sandys, *Ovid's Metamorphosis* ed. K. J. Hulley and S. Vandersall (Lincoln: University of Nebraska Press, 1970), p. 384)

Marlowe might have got the first hint from *EFB*, ch. 2 where the magician, 'taking to him the wings of an Eagle, thought to flie over the whole world'; but the Icarus myth was readily available—and had earlier been used by Marlowe in *Dido Queene of Carthage* when the desperate Dido plans to fly to Aeneas:

Ile frame me wings of waxe like *Icarus*.
And ore his ships will soare unto the Sunne,
That they may melt and I fall in his arms: (V. i. 243–5)

The falling Icarus was a popular Renaissance emblem, often bearing the warning *noli altum sapere*, throughout Europe—as Carlo Ginzburg shows in his essay 'High and Low: the Theme of Forbidden Knowledge in the Sixteenth and Seventeenth Centuries', *Past and Present*, lxxiii (1976), 28–41).

22 heavens conspirde his overthrow] Marlowe used the same expression in *1 Tamburlaine* when the conqueror boasts of the support of 'The chiefest God', who

> Will sooner burne the glorious frame of Heaven,
> Then it should so conspire my overthrow.   (IV. ii. 10–11)

23 falling to] The compound *fall to* (*OED* 66) has a range of meanings which include 'To be drawn by feeling to' (66a), 'To have recourse to' (66d), and 'To begin (eating or working)' (66e). The imagery in lines 24 ff. develops from this last usage.

25 Negromancy] The spelling of the A text shows a common etymological confusion of 'necromancy' (deriving from Greek νεκρος (nekros), a corpse, and referring to divination by means of communication with the dead) and 'nigromancy' (from the Latin *niger* = black). *EFB* seems to make a distinction, recording that Faustus 'gave himself secretly to study Necromancy and Conjuration'.

27 his chiefest blisse] *OED* comments on the relationship of *bless* and *bliss*, and the confusion of spelling which brought about 'the gradual tendency to withdraw *bliss* from earthly "blitheness" to the beatitude of the blessed in heaven'. A quotation from Wyclif (*bliss* 2c) illustrates the usage: 'He [the pope] is not blessid in this lyf, for bliss fallith to the tother lyf.'

28 this . . . sits] Presumably this line is the cue for the Chorus to draw aside a curtain and reveal '*Faustus in his study*' (as in the stage direction of the B text). Such a 'discovery' was a favourite opening, which Marlowe used at the beginning of *Dido Queene of Carthage*:

Here the Curtaines draw, there is discovered JUPITER *dandling* GANIMED *upon his knee, and* MERCURY *lying asleepe.*

The Prologue to *The Jew of Malta*, spoken by the choric figure of Machevil (Machiavelli) is comparable.

Scene 1

OSD *Enter . . . Study*] A direction which seems to indicate the use of some kind of inner acting area; the character is 'discovered' when the curtains are drawn back: cf. *The Jew of Malta*, '*Enter* BARABAS *in his*

Counting-house, with heapes of gold before him' (I. i. OSD), and *Othello*, '*Enter* OTHELLO *and* DESDEMONA *in her bed*' (V. ii. OSD).

2 To sound] 'To measure, or ascertain, as by sounding' *OED v²* 5; cf. the promise of Prospero at the end of *The Tempest*: 'deeper than did ever plummet sound | I'll drown my book' (V. i. 56–7).

2 professe] *OED* 5, 'claim to have expert knowledge of or skill in (some art or science)'.

3 commencde] Graduated as Doctor of Divinity (been 'grac't with doctors name'); at Cambridge the Congregation of Senate at which degrees are conferred is called Commencement.

4–37 every art . . . best] Faustus's survey of human scholarship has a counterpart in Lyly's *Euphues* (1578), where the protagonist decides to forsake the company of women and return to academe:

I will to *Athens* ther to tosse my bookes . . . Philosophie, Phisicke, Diuinitie, shal be my studie. O yᵉ hidden secrets of Nature, the expresse image of morall vertues, the equall ballaunce of Iustice, the medicines to heale all diseases, how they beginne to delyght me. The *Axiomaes* of *Aristotle*, the *Maxims* of *Iustinian*, the *Aphorismes* of *Galen*, haue sodaynelye made such a breache into my minde, that I seeme onely to desire them which did onely earst detest them. (John Lyly, *Euphues* (1578), in *The Complete Works of John Lyly*, ed. R. Warwick Bond (Oxford, 1902), 3 vols., i.241)

5 *Aristotles* workes] In the sixteenth century the university curriculum was based on the study of Aristotle, although his supremacy was disputed in Cambridge (while Marlowe was a student there) by the intellectual reformer Petrus Ramus. Marlowe knew Ramus's work (which he quotes here—line 7), and the circumstances of his assassination (which is presented in *The Massacre at Paris*).

6 *Analutikes*] An obvious misprint, *Anulatikes* in A1 is corrected in A2 to *Analitikes*; but Greg pointed out that the misspelling in A1 must have arisen from Marlowe's having written *Analutikes*; he compared the spelling *metem su cossis* (scene 13 line 102) which A3 corrects to *metemsycosis*. The *Analytica priora* and *posteriora* were two of the six treatises on logic which were later known as the *Organon*. Here Aristotle explored the science of reasoning, basing his argument on the syllogism—which he himself had discovered.

7 Bene . . . logicis] B4 corrects to the Greek genitive with *logices*, but the mistake probably originates with Marlowe, who is quoting the definition of Peter Ramus (see *note* to line 5) who wrote *finis Logicae, bene disserere* in *The First Booke of Dialecticke*; the English translation of 1574 opens with the statement 'Dialecticke otherwise called Logicke, is an arte which teachethe to dispute well.'

12 Oncaymaeon] The uncomprehending printer of A2 made his own sense of the jumble of letters, and printed *Oeconomy*; the reading was followed in the subsequent A3 and in the B text. Bullen recognized A1's word as transliteration of the Greek phrase ὄν καὶ μὴ ὄν (existent or non-existent), and Dr Peter Glare of Oxford University Press explained to me that the phrase 'appears to derive from Gorgias of Leontini (*c*.483–376 BC)'.

Galen] A second-century Greek physician, accepted as an authority on medical science throughout the Middle Ages.

13 Seeing . . . *medicus*] The adaptation of a sentence in Aristotle's *de sensu et sensibili*, ch. 1, 436a.

14 Be a physition] The association of gold and the medical profession is an old one: Shakespeare mentions the use of gold for 'Preserving life in med'cine potable' (*2 Henry IV*, IV. v. 162). Faustus, however, is mercenary—like Chaucer's Physician in *The Canterbury Tales*:

> For gold in phisik is a cordial,
> Therefore he lovede gold in special.   (Prologue, 444–5)

15 eternizde] Although sense 3 of *eternize* (= to immortalize, make perpetually famous) is not recorded until 1610 in *OED*, it was a favourite form with Marlowe: cf. *1 Tamburlaine*, I. ii. 72 ('as thou hop'st to be eternized') and *2 Tamburlaine*, V. i. 35 ('this eternisde citie *Babylon*').

16 *Summum . . . sanitas*] Translated by Faustus in the following line, this precept is latinized by Marlowe from Aristotle's *Nicomachean Ethics*, 1094. a. 8.

19 found Aphorismes] Faustus ranks himself with Hippocrates, whose *Aphorisms* was the most famous of medical textbooks. 'To have your words taken as aphorisms is clearly a triumph which many would desire', says Brian Vickers in the chapter on 'The Aphorism' in his *Francis Bacon and Renaissance Prose* (Cambridge: Cambridge University Press, 1968), p. 62. Vickers quotes Thomas Lodge, who attacked the vanity of his allegorical character 'Boasting' (*Wits Miserie*, 1596) for aspiring to the authority of a Faustus:

Though he looke with a counterfait eie, none must see further than he, and whatsoever he saith, must be held an Aphorisme, or he flings house out of the window with his boastings.

Lodge's 'held as' supports the emendation from *sound* to *found*; A's error can be explained by the compositor's mistaking of a long *s* for *f*. The line is omitted in the B text.

20 billes] *OED sb.*[3]5b offers 1529 for the earliest use of *bill* to mean 'medical prescription': 'After the billes made by the great physicion God,

prescrybynge the medicines himself' (Sir Thomas More). *OED* also cites a couplet from *Hudibras* (1663) referring to

> him that took the Doctor's Bill,
> And swallow'd it instead o'th'Pill.

20–1 hung . . . plague] The syntax is rather compressed. The prescriptions ('billes') have been preserved in recognition of the fact that their agency (i.e. the agency of the drugs prescribed) has been effective.

21 plague] Christopher Ricks wrote of the bubonic plague which is part of the social context of *Dr Faustus*: 'the plague is not Marlowe's subject but his environment and element' ('*Dr Faustus* and Hell on Earth', *Essays in Criticism*, xxxv (1985), 101–20).

24 Couldst] (A 'wouldst'); B's emendation is justifiable only on the grounds of common sense. Faustus craves the divine power to grant eternal life, or the power of Christ, who raised Lazarus from the dead (St John 2: 1–44). A's printer seems to be unusually careless with this speech.

men] A's *man* might have been caught up from the preceding line; the *them* in line 25 supports B's correction.

27 *Justinian*] A Roman emperor of the sixth century AD, chiefly remarkable for having reorganized the whole of Roman law. His *Corpus Juris* consisted of four parts, the first of which was *Institutiones*, a manual intended for the use of students.

28–9 *Si una . . . rei*] 'If one and the same thing is bequeathed to two individuals, one of them shall have the thing itself, and the other the value of the thing'; Faustus seems to be recollecting the ruling given in II. xx. 8 of the *Institutiones*:

Si eadem res duobus legata sit sive coniunctim sive disiunctim, si ambo perveniant ad legatum, scinditur inter eos legatum: si alter deficiat, quia aut spreverit legatum aut vivo testatore decesserit aut alio quolibet modo defecerit, totum ad collegatarium pertinet.

('If the same thing be left to two people, whether conjunctively or disjunctively, and both come to take the legacy, it is shared between them; if one fails to take, because he refuses or dies during the testator's life or for any other reason, the whole goes to his co-legatee.') (*The Institutes of Justinian*, ed. J. A. C. Thomas (Oxford, 1975), p. 141)

In modernized texts, Dyce's emendation to *legatur* corrects the Latin.

30 pretty] A's dismissive irony is lost in the tautology of the B text reading: 'a pettie case of paltry legacies'.

31 *Ex . . . nisi*] 'A father cannot disinherit his son unless . . .'. Justinian deals with 'the Disherison of Issue' in II. xiii of the *Institutiones*;

Faustus may be misremembering the phraseology of one of the exclusion clauses:

Nominatim autem exheredari quis videtur sive ita exheredetur TITIUS FILIUS MEUS EXHERES ESTO . . . (*Institutes*, ed. J. A. C. Thomas, p. 119).

32 institute] i.e. Justinian's *Institutiones* (see *note* to line 27).

33 body of the law] The *Corpus Juris* of Justinian. A's error 'Church' is difficult to explain.

34 This study] Greg suggests that A's reading, if not an error, might refer back to 'Justinian'.

36 Too servile] A 'The devill'; of the variant reading Greg writes 'How this admitted nonsense got into A is hard to guess, but it is no worse than that in [33]. There is, of course, some graphic resemblance, but it is slight.'

illiberal] Milton explains in *Animadversions* (1642) that 'Not liberal science, but illiberal must that needs be that mounts in contemplation meerely for money' (*Complete Prose Works of John Milton*, ed. D. M. Wolfe *et al.* (New Haven: Yale University Press, 1953–82), i. 720).

38 *Jeromes* Bible] The Vulgate, the Latin Bible (*editio vulgata*) most widely used in the West; it was the work of St Jerome, who compiled it at the command of the pope in the fourth century.

39–45 *Stipendium* . . . consequently die] Trained in the syllogistic reasoning of Aristotle (see *note* to line 5), Dr Faustus demonstrates his technique. Jump observes that 'There is nothing subversive of Christian doctrine in a syllogism which shows that man is condemned by the letter of the law. What is unorthodox is Faustus's refusal to see that man, thus condemned, may be redeemed by the sacrifice of Christ.'

39 *Stipendium* . . . *est*] From the Epistle to the Romans, 6: 23: *Stipendium enim peccati, mors.*

&c] Greg observes that this 'seems to be a direction for repetition: Faustus murmurs the words over to himself, his voice dying away'. It is certainly *not* an indication that Faustus should appear to continue his reading in the Epistle to the Romans, where the second half of verse 23 explains that 'the gift of God is eternal life through Jesus Christ our Lord'.

41 *Si* . . . *veritas*] From the First Epistle General of John, 1: 8: *Si dixerimus quoniam peccatum non habemus, ipsi non seducimus, et veritas in nobis non est.* Instead of using the Vulgate himself, Marlowe seems to be offering his own Latin versions of an English text. The next verse of this Epistle (like the second part of Romans 6: 23) could have solved the doctor's dilemma: 'If we confess our sins, he is faithful and just to forgive us our sins, and to cleanse us from all unrighteousness.'

42–3 If . . . us] Although these lines are printed as verse in both A and B texts, it is quite clear, as Greg said, that 'at this point Faustus suddenly lapses into prose . . . The effect is calculated: for a moment the world reels as the foundations of religion give way beneath him. And it makes effective the return to verse at [44]'. Faustus's English quotation is not taken from the Bible directly, but from the 1559 Book of Common Prayer, where the sentence is used to preface the exhortation to repentance; this is immediately followed by the order for General Confession.

47 *Che sera, sera*] An Italian proverb; *sera* is an early form of *sara*, and is accented on the second syllable.

48 What . . . be] The king in *Edward II* bows to inevitability with much the same words: 'Wel, that shalbe, shalbe' (IV. vii. 95).

adieu] With a pun, Divinity is given over to God (*à Dieu*). *EFB* is the source for the impatience: 'sometime he would throw the Scriptures from him as though he had no care of his former profession . . . in so much that hee could not abide to bee called Doctor of Divinitie'.

49 Metaphisickes] 'Used for occult and magical lore'; *OED* cites this line as its only instance for *metaphysics* 2. In its more usual sense (*OED* 1), *metaphysics* is 'The branch of speculative inquiry that treats of the first principles of things, including such concepts as being, substance, essence, time, space, cause, identity, *etc.*' Cf. *2 Tamburlaine*, IV. ii. 63–4, where Olympia claims to have an ointment 'Tempered by science metaphisicall, | And Spels of magicke from the mouthes of spirits'.

50 Negromantike] Cf. Prologue line 25, and *note*.

51 Lines, circles] Dr Faustus is fascinated by the *technique* of conjuring. The 'Lines' are explained by Ormerod and Wortham as those 'used in geomancy, the art of divination by means of signs derived from the earth'; cf. Francis Sparr's translation of *Cattan's Geomancie* (1591), 1: 'Geomancie is a Science and Art which consisteth of points, prickes, and lines, made in steade of the foure elements.' The *circle* (*OED* 3) was much used as a figure of magic or necromancy: within its confines the magician was protected from any evil spirit that responded to his conjuration—the title-page of the 1616 *Dr Faustus* illustrates the magician's circle (see p. 107).

schemes] A has 'scenes', which B (and many modern editors) dismisses as apparently unintelligible. Helen Gardner, however, found the same misreading in manuscripts of Donne's elegy, 'The Bracelet', where the line (printed correctly in the edition of 1633) describes the conjuror 'Which with fantastique schemes fullfills much paper' (60). Helen Gardner explains that ' "Schema" and "Figura" are interchangeable terms in magical works.' A *scheme* (*OED* 2) is a 'diagram showing the relative positions, either real or apparent, of the heavenly bodies'.

letters and characters] Dr Faustus explains these himself in scene 3, lines 8–13.

55 Artizan] *OED* describes as '*Obs.*' the sense (1) which it illustrates with this usage: 'One who practises, or cultivates, an art'.

56 quiet poles] The north and south poles; they are 'quiet' because they are motionless.

Nor ... cloudes] Unmistakable signs of supernatural power. When Christ calmed the storm on the Sea of Galilee, 'the men marvelled, saying, What manner of man is this, that even the winds and the sea obey him?' (St Matthew 27: 1). Prospero attained to the skills that Faustus desires, claiming at the end of *The Tempest* that, with the aid of spirits, he had

> bedimm'd
> The noontide sun, call'd forth the mutinous winds,
> And 'twixt the green sea and the azur'd vault
> Set roaring war.   (V. i. 41–4)

The line is omitted in the B text.

60 exceedes] *OED* offers *exceed* 5, 'To be preeminent, whether in a good or a bad sense'.

62 a mighty god] With characteristic caution the editor of the B text, fearing the strictures of the Act of Abuses, modified this to 'a Demi-god'. Approving B against what he called A's 'characteristic exaggeration', Greg remarked 'Goethe's instinct was right: Du hast sie zerstört, Die schöne Welt, mit mächtiger Faust: Ein Halbgott hat sie zerschlagen! [You have destroyed it, this beautiful world, with a mighty fist. A demi-god has shattered it!]'

deerest friends] The identity of these two has not been discovered.

69 SD EVILL ANGELL] B introduces this creature simply as 'Spirit' (= devil); see *note* to scene 5 line 97.

82 *India*] *OED* cites *Purchas his Pilgrimage* (1614) to illustrate the confusion of senses of *India*: 'The name of India, is now applied to all farre-distant Countries, not in the extreme limits of Asia alone; but even to whole America, through the errour of Columbus ... who ... in the Westerne world, thought that they had met with Ophir, and the Indian regions of the East.'

83 orient] *OED* distinguishes between the pearl found in the Indian seas and those, less beautiful, from European oysters (*orient* 2b).

88 wall ... brasse] Dr Faustus plans to emulate Greene's Friar Bacon who determined to use his supernatural powers to 'circle England round with brass' (*Friar Bacon and Friar Bungay* (*c.*1589), scene 2 line 29).

Friar Bacon and Dr Faustus both perhaps hoped to equal Spenser's Merlin:

> Before that *Merlin* dyde, he did intend
> A brasen wall in compass to compile,
> About *Cairmardin* . . .
>   (*The Faerie Queene*, III. iii. 10)

89 swift *Rhine* . . . *Wertenberge*] Wittenberg in fact stands on the river Elbe.

90–91] fill . . . clad] Dyce's emendation to 'silk' (A reads 'skill') can best be understood in Marlowe's Cambridge context. The 'publike schooles' are the university (not the college) lecture-rooms; and Cambridge undergraduates were ordered to dress soberly. Lyly (an Oxford graduate) describes the students of 'Athens' (= Oxford) in *Euphues*:

haue they not nowe in steede of blacke cloth blacke veluet, in steede of course sackecloth fine silke? Be they not more like courtiers then schollers, more like stageplayers then students . . . (*Euphues*, ed. Bond, i. 274)

93 Prince of *Parma*] From 1579 until 1592 the Prince of Parma was Spanish governor-general of the United Provinces of the Netherlands. Dr Faustus derives his interest in the Low Countries from Marlowe, and not from the *EFB*. Marlowe himself was arrested in Flushing in 1592, when he was accused of fraudulent currency dealing, and deported to England; see R. B. Wernham, 'Christopher Marlowe in Flushing in 1592', *English Historical Review*, xci (1976), 344–5.

95 brunt] *OED* 2, 'assault, attack'.

96 fiery keele . . . bridge] On 4 April 1585 the Netherlanders used a fireship to make a breach in the bridge which Parma had built across the Scheldt to complete the blockade of Antwerp.

103–5 Yet not . . . skill] These lines are omitted in the B text. Cf. *EFB* ch. 1 (Appendix A) 'Doctor Faustus . . . fell into such fantasies and deep cogitations, that he was marked of many.'

108–9 Divinitie . . . vilde] These lines are omitted in the B text, presumably for fear of the 1606 legislation.

112 Consis sylogismes] A's printer set an apparently meaningless word 'Consissyllogismes' which the printer of A3 clarified into 'subtile sylogismes'; the B text perpetuated the reading of A3.

113 Graveld] *OED gravel* 4 (= perplex); cf. *As You Like It*: 'when you were gravell'd for lack of matter, you might take occasion to kiss' (IV. i. 76).

115 Problemes] *OED problem* 2, 'A question proposed for academic discussion or scholastic disputation'; more specifically, it is the term used in logic for the question in a syllogism.

116 *Musaeus . . .* hell] Hell is here confounded with the Elysian fields of *Aeneid* VI, where Musaeus holds a central place amongst the *felices animae* of patriots, priests, and bards. Virgil's Musaeus is not the author of *Hero and Leander* but a much earlier (*c.*1410 BC) poet, none of whose work is extant.

117 *Agrippa*] Henry Cornelius Agrippa von Nettesheim (1486–1535). In *The Unfortunate Traveller* (1594) Nashe refers to 'that abundant scholar' and his performances at Wittenberg before the scholars (who asked to see Plautus, Ovid, and Tully); at the imperial court he showed 'the whole destruction of Troy', and to entertain Lord Cromwell 'in a perspective glasse hee set before his eyes king *Henrie* the eight with all his Lordes on hunting in his forrest at Windsore'. For the delight of the emperor, Charles V, Agrippa 'shewed the nine worthies, *David*, *Salomon*, *Gedeon*, and the rest, in that similitude and likenes that they lived upon earth' (McKerrow, ii. 252–4).

121 Moores] In the sixteenth century this could refer to any dark-skinned race; the reference to '*Spanish* Lords' makes it clear that natives of the American continent are intended.

122 spirits] A's reading 'subjects' would appear to be an erroneous attempt by the compositor to carry on the sense of the preceding line. B is undoubtedly correct, referring to such beings as 'the spirits that pyromancy calls' and the 'geomantic fiends' which, according to the discussion of their various skills in Greene's *Friar Bacon and Friar Bungay*, 'do serve For jugglers, witches, and vild sorcerers' (scene 9).

125 *Almaine . . .* staves] Lance-bearing German cavalry.

126 *Lapland* Gyants] Orcanes in *2 Tamburlaine* describes

> Vast *Gruntland* compast with the frozen sea,
> Inhabited with tall and sturdy men,
> Gyants as big as hugie *Polypheme*. (I. i. 26–8)

128 in the] A's 'in their' would seem to be caught up from the preceding line; B offers the clumsy 'has the' in an effort to make sense.

130 From . . . dragge] A2 corrects the anticipatory error of A1's 'From', and the obvious misprint in 'dregge'.

Argoces] The *Ragusa* was the largest size of Venetian merchant vessel (cf. *OED argosy*); the word was easily linked (at least in Marlowe's mind) with the name of the ship, the *Argo*, in which Jason and 'the vent'rous youth of Greece' (*Hero and Leander*, line 57) sailed to Colchis in search of the golden fleece of the ram that carried Helle and her brother Phryxus when they escaped from Thebes.

131–2 from *America* . . . treasury] Marlowe refers to the annual plate-fleet which brought the American tribute to Spain; 'stuffes' became 'stuff'd' in the B text as that edition's editor recognized the death (in 1598) of Philip II.

138–9 He that is . . . minerals] *EFB* (ch. 1) tells how Faustus 'accompanied himselfe with divers that were seene in those divelish Arts, and that had the *Chaldean*, *Persian*, *Hebrew*, *Arabian*, and *Greeke* tongues . . . and named himselfe an Astrologian'. The *lingua franca* of Renaissance scholars, Latin, was essential for communication with spirits—which is why Horatio was called upon to address the Ghost in Hamlet: 'Thou art a scholar, speak to it Horatio' (I. i. 43). To be conversant with ('well seene in') the properties of minerals was particularly necessary for the alchemical magician.

143 the *Delphian* Oracle] The oracular shrine of Apollo in his temple at Delphi, which was the supreme authority in classical Greece for most matters of religion and morality. A1 reads 'Dolphian', but the evident misprint was corrected in A2.

147 massie] *OED* 1, 'Full of substance or "mass" '.

151 lustie] The sense (*OED* 2) of *lusty*, meaning 'pleasant, agreeable', was available to Marlowe at the end of the sixteenth century; but it quickly became obsolete: in A2 and 3 the word was changed to 'little', and the editor of B substituted 'bushy'.

154 wise *Bacons* and *Albanus* workes] The first of these was Roger Bacon, a Franciscan friar of the thirteenth century, whose varied expertise earned him the title of *Doctor Mirabilis*: in the Renaissance he was popularly thought of as a magician (and was one of the eponymous heroes of Greene's *Friar Bacon and Friar Bungay*). The name of Albertus Magnus, a German Dominican philosopher and experimental scientist, is sometimes linked with Bacon's; but it is probable that Marlowe is here referring to Pietro d'Abano (*c*.1250–1316), an Italian humanist physician who was also believed to have been a conjuror.

155 The Hebrew Psalter, and new Testament] In his *Discovery of Witchcraft* (1584), Reginald Scot recommends Psalms 22 and 51, and the opening verses of St John's Gospel, as being especially efficacious for conjuration (Book XV, ch. 14).

159 all other ceremonies] *EFB* (ch. 1) refers to the 'ceremonies belonging to these infernal Arts, as Necromancie, Charmes, Southsaying, Witchcraft, Inchantment'.

161 rudiments] James VI and I in his *Daemonologie* (Edinburgh, 1597)

scathingly dismissed 'all that which is called vulgarly the vertue of worde, herbe, & stone: which is used by unlawful charmes, without natural causes ... such kinde of charmes as commonlie daft wives use' (p. 11).

164 canvass every quidditie] Explore every detail; *quidditie* is a scholastic term denoting the essence of a thing, that which makes it what it is.

Scene 2

2 *sic probo*] 'Thus I prove it'; the triumphant cry of the disputing scholar was turned into a generic name for scholars by Thomas Nashe in *Pierce Penilesse His Supplication to the Divell* (1592): 'it is no matter what *Sic probo* and his pennilesse companions prate' (McKerrow, i. 160).

3 his boy] *EFB* describes (ch. 56) how Faustus:

had a prety stripling to his servant, the which had studied also at the Universitie of Wittenberg: this youth was very well acquainted with his knaveries and sorceries, so that hee was hated as well for his owne knaveries, as also for his Masters: for no man would give him entertainement into his service, because of his unhappines, but Faustus: this Wagner was so well beloved of Faustus, that hee used him as his sonne ...'.

11 licentiats] Graduates—the holders of a degree between bachelor and doctor; these Scholars are probably bachelors *in statu pupillari*.

13–16 Why ... thiefe] This seems to have been the formula for some kind of stock theatrical 'business'; it was so popular as to be considered worthy of an entry in M. P. Tilley's *Dictionary of Proverbs in England in the Sixteenth and Seventeenth Centuries* (Ann Arbor: University of Michigan Press, 1950), F. 177: 'ask my fellow (companion) if I be a thief'.

18 dunces] The term of abuse was originally applied to the followers of Duns Scotus (d.1308), who were notorious for the kind of quibbling logic that Wagner himself is demonstrating; by the end of the sixteenth century the insult was being used more generally to impute old-fashioned pedantry resistant to new ideas.

20 *corpus naturale ... mobile*] 'A natural body and [therefore] capable of movement'—the current academic definition of the subject-matter of physics.

23–4 fortie foote ... execution] Nashe uses the same expression in *Strange Newes* (1592) when he warns the readers to avoid Harvey's wrath and 'stand fortie foote from the execution place of his furie' (McKerrow, i. 281).

26 precisian] One who is rigidly precise in observing the rules for conduct; in the sixteenth century the word was synonymous with 'puritan'—

and Wagner now apes the unctuous speech forms of the religious puritans.

32–8 Nay then . . . do] In the B text the Scholars have the following verse sequence:

> 1 SCH. O *Faustus*, then I feare that which I have long suspected:
> That thou art falne into that damned Art
> For which they two are infamous through the world.
> 2 SCH. Were he a stranger, not allyed to me,
> The danger of his soule would make me mourne:
> But come, let us go, and informe the *Rector*:
> It may be his grave counsell may reclaime him.
> 1 SCH. I feare me, nothing will reclaime him now.
> 2 SCH. Yet let us see what we can do.

36 the Rector] *EFB* alludes in this way to the head of the University of Wittenberg.

Scene 3

For the *EFB* version of this scene see Appendix A, ch. 2.

0 SD Enter . . . *conjure*] The B text enlarges on this direction, reading *Thunder. Enter Lucifer and 4. devils. Faustus to them with this speech.*

1–4 Now . . . breath] The anonymous author of *The Taming of A Shrew* (SR 1594) stole these lines for his own play, but replaced Marlowe's 'shadow of the earth' with the pleonastic 'shadow of the night'. His version was copied in the B text, and many subsequent editors have chosen this reading for *Dr Faustus*. However, John Norton Smith in 'Marlowe's "Faustus"' (*Notes and Queries*, NS 25, 5 (1978), 436–7) explains the complicated mixture of pre-Copernican scientific fact and Marlovian mythopeic imagining which is condensed into this short passage. He cites the authority of Macrobius to explain that 'night is the result of the casting upwards of the earth's shadow after the sun has vacated the upper hemisphere'. The 'pitchy breath' needs a note from Lucretius' *De Rerum Natura* (iv. 476 ff.), describing the vapours and fumes of the night which 'fill up the sky with their blackness'. Marlowe invents a new myth, rooted in the old science, when he hints at the love of the earth's shadow for the watery star, *nimbosus* Orion. Darkness also comes quickly in *Lucans First Booke*, where Marlowe speaks of 'th'earths suddaine shadow' (line 537), and another rapid sunset is described in *2 Tamburlaine*:

> When *Phoebus* leaping from his Hemi-Spheare,
> Discendeth downeward to th'Antipodes.

(I. ii. 51–2)

The constellation Orion appears in northern latitudes at the beginning of winter, usually heralding rain—hence the appellations *nimbosus* and *aquosus* in the *Aeneid* (i. 535 and iv. 52).

8 Within this circle] i.e. on the circumference of the magic circle whose confines protected the magician; the title-page of the B text provides an illustration (p. 107).

Jehovahs name] The tetragrammaton, the four-lettered Hebrew word which was too sacred for the Jews to utter, and which is usually rendered in English as 'Yahweh'.

10 The breviated] *OED* gives *breviate* as a recognized aphetic form of *abbreviate*; it was sufficiently rare, however, to trouble the B text editor, who instead offered 'Th'abreviated'.

11 Figures of every adjunct to the heavens] *OED figure* 14, 'A scheme or table showing the disposition of the heavens at any given time'. Heavenly bodies (other than the planets) were conceived of as being joined to the solid firmament of the sky.

12 And . . . starres] Astrological symbols for the signs of the zodiac, and for the planets—which were 'erring [i.e. wandering] starres' because they were not joined to the firmament (unlike the 'fixed stars').

13 spirits are inforst to rise] Many neoplatonic philosophers—including Marsilio Ficino (*De triplici vita*, 1489)—believed that spirits could be attracted, or even compelled, to visit the magician who employed the proper skills and spells. Agrippa, in *De occulta philosophia* (1510), distinguished two kinds of magic, theurgic magic (whose spirits were docile and servile), and goetic magic, which did indeed involve diabolic powers (that were likely to enslave the magician).

16–22 *Sint . . . Mephastophilis*] 'May the gods of the underworld look favourably upon me. Farewell to the threefold deity of Jehovah: and hail, you spirits of fire, air and water. Prince of the East, Beelzebub the king of burning hell, and Demogorgon, grant us that grace, that Mephastophilis may appear and rise up. What do you hesitate for? By Jehovah, Gehenna, and the power of the holy water which I now sprinkle, and the sign of the cross which I now make, and by our vows, may Mephastophilis now arise at our command.'

16 *acherontis*] Acheron was one of the rivers of the Greek underworld; and the rhetorical figure of metonymy takes the part for the whole.

numen triplex Jehovae] The Holy Trinity—the Christian God in Three Persons: Father, Son, and Holy Ghost. Faustus dismisses one triune God in order to invoke the infernal trilogy of Lucifer, Beelzebub, and Demogorgon.

17 *Aquatani*] Tucker Brooke and Bowers correct the Latin to *Aquatici*;

Greg, Jump, and Bowers include the spirit of earth in the invocation by adding *Terreni*.

17–18 *Orientis . . . demogorgon*] In Isaiah 12:14 Lucifer, the light-bringer, is apostrophized as 'sun of the morning'—and *Orientis princeps* would be a more fitting title for him than for Beelzebub, to whom it is given in the A text by a misplaced comma. In Matthew 12:24 Beelzebub is referred to as 'prince of devils', and in the hierarchy of *Paradise Lost* Milton locates him very close to Lucifer:

> by his side
> One next himself in power, and next in crime,
> Long after known in Palestine, and named
> Beelzebub. (i. 78–81)

Ancient mythology recognized Demogorgon as one of the most terrible primeval gods, whose very name brought death and disaster. Milton refers to 'the dreaded name of Demogorgon" (*Paradise Lost*, ii. 966), and in Book VI of the *Pharsalia* Lucan speaks of the god:

> At whose dread name the trembling furies quake,
> Hell stands abashed, and earth's foundations shake.
> (translated by N. Rowe, London, 1718)

19 *Mephastophilis*] This seems to be Marlowe's preferred spelling of the name—it is the most frequent in the A text, although there are variants such as 'Mephostophilis' and 'Mephastophilus'. *EFB* calls the devil 'Mephostophiles'. In chapter 5 of the source book, the spirit explains that he is 'a prince, but servant to Lucifer'. At this point in the invocation the B text inserts the English word 'Dragon'; and this has given rise to considerable academic bewilderment. In 1598 the Admiral's Men listed among their stage properties 'i dragon in fostes' (Henslowe, p. 320) and it is generally assumed that this object is referred to. Boas and Greg both accepted that the stage performance would attempt to recreate the episode in *EFB* when Faustus's conjuration is (without his noticing) instantly rewarded: 'sodainly over his head hanged hovering in the ayre a mighty Dragon' (ch. 2). Kirschbaum, however, suggested an anticipatory stage direction—a warning to the book-keeper to prepare the property dragon for its entry at line 22, where it could be presented as the required 'Divel' (Leo Kirschbaum, 'The Good and Bad Quartos of *Dr Faustus*', *The Library*, xxvi (March 1946), 272–94).

19 *quid tu moraris*] why do you delay? Boas corrected the Q reading—*tumeraris*—which is common to both A and B. *EFB* tells how 'Faustus all this while [was] halfe amazed at the Divels so long tarrying' (ch. 2).

20 *gehennam*] Gehenna, the Valley of Hinnom, was a place of sacrifice and, in the words of *Paradise Lost*, 'the type of hell' (i. 404).

21 *per vota nostra*] The most important vows for a Christian are the ones made at his baptism—promises to renounce the world, the flesh, and the devil.

23 chaunge thy shape] The dragon in Marlowe's source turns (of its own volition) into a 'fiery globe' which in turn changes into a 'fiery man'; 'This pleasant beast ranne about the circle a great while, and lastly appeared in manner of a gray Frier, asking Faustus what was his request' (ch. 2).

32 Conjuror laureate] The laurel wreath of excellence was given to poets in ancient Greece; the tradition was continued in England by the universities of Oxford and Cambridge, and it survives in the title of the 'poet laureate'.

35–54 Now . . . hell.] In *EFB* this conversation does not take place until Faustus has returned to his house; cf. Appendix A, ch. 3.

44 mine owne accord] What P. H. Kocher calls 'the doctrine of voluntary ascent' is fairly well established in witchcraft; cf. Paul H. Kocher, *Christopher Marlowe* (Chapel Hill, NC, 1946), p. 160.

46 yet *per accident*] The conjuring speeches *were* the cause—but only in appearance. A logical accident is some quality or property which a thing possesses, but which is not essential to it. The invocation was the effective cause of the devil's appearance; but the real cause was the state of mind that prompted Faustus to his conjuring.

53 the Trinitie] The B text plays for safety here with 'all godlinesse'.

56 *Belsibub*] The apparent confusion of diabolic personages originates in the Bible, where the 'chiefe' of the devils is variously referred to as Lucifer, Beelzebub, and Satan.

59 confounds hell in *Elizium*] In his Preface to Greene's *Menaphon* (1589) Nashe speaks dismissively of the 'home borne mediocritie' of writers 'that thrust *Elisium* into hell', i.e. make no distinction between hell and the Greek world of the afterlife (McKerrow, iii. 316).

60 olde Philosophers] Marlowe translates a line from one of those same philosophers, Averroes, who shared Faustus's disbelief in an eternity of torment: *sit anima mea cum philosophis.* Cf. J. C. Maxwell, *Notes and Queries*, cxiv (1949), 334–5; and J. M. Steadman, *Notes and Queries*, ccvii (1962), 327–9.

62 that *Lucifer*] A simple account of the history of Lucifer is given in Isaiah 14: 12–15, where the prophet exclaims:

How art thou fallen from heaven, O Lucifer, son of the morning . . .
For thou hast said in thine heart, I will ascend into heaven, I will exalt my throne above the stars of God . . .

I will ascend above the heights of clouds; I will be like the most High.
Yet thou shalt be brought down to hell, to the sides of the pit.

Milton describes the residual grandeur of the fallen angel in *Paradise Lost*, i. 589–594:

> he above the rest
> In shape and gesture proudly eminent
> Stood like a tower; his form had not yet lost
> All her original brightness, nor appeared
> Less than archangel ruined, and the excess
> Of glory obscured.

69–72 And what . . . with *Lucifer*] These four lines form the rhetorical figure known to Peacham as *epiphora*—'when many members or clauses, doe ende still with one and the same word' (*The Garden of Eloquence* (1577), sig. I, 1ᵛ).

74 In hell] Caxton, while locating hell 'in the most lowest place, most derke, and most vyle of the erthe', stressed that it is a state as well as a place; the soul condemned to hell is like a man 'that had a grete maladye, so moche that he shold deye, and that he were brought in to a fair place and plesaunt for to have Joye and solace; of so moche shold he be more hevy and sorowful' (*The Mirrour of the World* (1480), ii. 18). The same concept is expressed eloquently in *Paradise Lost*, where Milton describes the ubiquity of Satan's hell:

> within him hell
> He brings, and round about him, nor from hell
> One step no more than from himself can fly
> By change of place. (iv. 20–3)

79–80 tormented . . . blisse] Mephastophilis's account of the torment of deprivation is translated from St John Chrysostom: *si decem mille gehennas quis dixerit, nihil tale est quale ab illa beata visione excidere*; see John Searle, letter to *The Times Literary Supplement*, 15 February 1936.

87 these] A's reading 'those' (corrected in B) is an obvious error, arising probably from a repetition of the preceding line.

91 foure and twentie] For the sake of the rhythm, it is useful to follow the example of A3 and expand A1's '24'.

102 Had . . . starres] Jump suggests a comparison with Addition 5 of *The Spanish Tragedy*:

> Had I as many lives as there be stars,
> As many heavens to go to as those lives,
> I'd give them all, aye, and my soul to boot,
> But I would see thee ride in this red pool.

106 To passe . . . men] Faustus aims to emulate Xerxes, who built a bridge (using boats) across the Hellespont for his army of seven hundred thousand men.

107 the hills . . . shore] The hills on either side of the Straits of Gibraltar which, if joined, would unite Africa and Europe into a single continent.

Scene 4

I discussed this scene at length in ' "Such conceits as clownage keeps in pay": comedy and *Dr Faustus*', in *The Fool and The Trickster*, ed. P. V. A. Williams (Thetford: Brewer, 1979), pp. 55–63. The B text version of the scene, which has been heavily cut to remove the cruder comic elements, is printed in Appendix B, p. 108. There is nothing in *EFB* to correspond with scene 4, although there is perhaps a hint for the character of Wagner in chapter 56 (see Appendix A).

1–3 Sirra boy . . . as I have] The anonymous *The Taming of A Shrew* duplicates this opening in the exchange (sig. C4ᵛ) between the 'Boy' and the clown, Sander:

> BOY. Come hither sirha boy.
> SAN[DER]. Boy; oh disgrace to my person, souns boy
> Of your face, you haue many boies with such
> Pickadeuantes I am sure . . .

The editor of the B text chose to follow the version in *A Shrew*.

3 pickadevaunts] The small pointed beard (*pic à devant*) was fashionable at the end of the sixteenth century; in *The Unfortunate Traveller* (1594) Nashe describes the university orator 'whose pickerdevant was verie plentifully besprinkled with rose water' (McKerrow, ii. 246). By 1616 the style had perhaps lost its novelty—hence the substitution of 'beards' in the B text.

15 *Qui mihi discipulus*] 'You who are my pupil'—the opening words of a didactic Latin poem by the schoolmaster William Lily. The poem would be familiar to every Elizabethan schoolboy; cf. Madido's description of his early education in *Pilgrimage to Parnassus* (performed 1598/9): 'I tooke shipping at *Qui mihi discipulus* & sailed to *Propria quae maribus*, then came to *As in praesenti*' (II. i. 229 ff.).

17 beaten . . . staves acre] 'In effect Wagner promises to dress his servant (or rather to dress him down) in silk—and adds that plenty of Keating's powder will be needed' (Greg). Gold was hammered into silk as a kind of embroidery; *stavesacre* was a preparation from delphinium seeds used for killing fleas.

18 knaves acre] Boas says that this was 'a mean street in London, more particularly Poultney Street, Soho'. This form of humour was outdated by the time of Shakespeare's *Two Gentlemen of Verona* (*c.*1594–5), where Speed seems weary when Launce refuses to distinguish between 'Mastership' and 'Master's ship': 'Well, your old vice still: mistake the word' (III. i. 285). The Clown in *Dr Faustus* continues his game with 'Gridyrons' in line 32.

33 *french* crownes] The Elizabethan chronicler, William Harrison, vouches for the topicality (and familiarity) of this joke when he writes in his *Description of England* (1587) that French and Flemish crowns are 'onlie currant among us, so long as they hold weight' (Book II, ch. xxv). There are no overtones here of the kind that Shakespeare plays with in *Measure for Measure* (1604), when Lucio's reference to 'A French crowne' brings from the First Gentleman the immediate response 'Thou art always figuring diseases in me' (I. ii. 49).

35 *english* counters] The French crowns (which were legal tender in England in the sixteenth century) were easily counterfeited; Marlowe himself is reported in the Baines' Libel as having boasted 'That he had as good Right to Coine as the Queen of England and that ... he ment, through the help of a Cunninge stamp maker to Coin ffrench Crownes pistoletes and English shillinges'. Among government measures to stop the flood of false coins was a proclamation of 1587 urging all who were offered such pieces to strike a hole in them (see Ruding, *Annals of the Coinage of Britain* (1817), i. 192 ff.); perhaps the Clown refers to the holes in the coins when he speaks of them as 'Gridyrons'.

39 take ... againe] this play with the coins is repeated in the anonymous *The Taming of a Shrew* (scene viii) where Sanders starts with 'Here here take your two shillings again'.

45 *Baliol*] A corruption of 'Belial'—'than whom a spirit more lewd Fell not from heaven' (*Paradise Lost*, i. 489–90); 'Belcher' is probably a similar mispronunciation of 'Beelzebub'.

48–50 kill one of them ... parish over] In *A Looking Glass for London*, written by Thomas Lodge and Robert Greene, and printed in 1594 (SR 5 March), the Clown attacks the devil who has come to carry him to hell. The devil pleads that he is mortally wounded, and the Clown triumphs with the boast:

Then may I count my selfe I thinke a tall man, that am able to kill a diuell. Now who dare deale with me in the parish, or what wench in *Ninivie* will not loue me, when they say, there goes he that beate the diuell. (G3ᵛ)

A Looking Glass was performed by Strange's Men in the spring of 1592.

49 round slop] Perhaps these baggy trousers (which were worn also by the Clown in *A Looking Glass for London*) became, thus early, a traditional costume for the stage clown.

63 frisking flea] A flea is the object of the poet's envy in the medieval *Carmen de Pulice* because it has freedom of access to all parts of his mistress's body. (See Commentary on scene 5 line 293.)

71 diametarily] *diametrally* is a parallel formation to the more common *diametrically*.

71-2 *vestigias nostras insistere*] The phrase is almost Virgilian—cf. *Aeneid* vii. 690 (*vestigia . . . instituere*) and xi. 574 (*vestigia . . . institerat*). Greg, remarking the similarity, objected that *The Aeneid* 'is of course poetry and the sense is that of planting one's feet rather than of following in the steps of another'. But Wagner's appropriation of the phrase is still comic.

73 *Dutch* fustian] A modern equivalent would be 'double Dutch'—i.e. gibberish or jargon; *fustian* is a coarse cloth made up of cotton and flax.

Scene 5

This, the central scene in the play, is based on material found at the heart of *EFB*—chapters 3–20.

9 I . . . againe] The censorship of the B text has cut out line 9, and replaced the question 'To God?' in line 10 with the exclamation 'Why'.

21 and of wealth] The absence of the word 'of' in A1 could be a simple misprint, quickly corrected in A2 and 3.

23 signory of *Emden*] Embden, at the mouth of the River Ems, was the chief town in East Friesland, at this time trading extensively with England.

25 God] B dilutes to the weak 'power'.

29 *Mephastophile*] A Latin vocative may be intended—which is appropriate enough where (as here in line 28) the *us* ending is preferred for the name of Mephastophilis.

31 he lives] The reading of the A text ('I live') is patently in need of this correction from B.

40 Inlarge his kingdome] 'Satan's chiefest drift & main point that he aimeth at, is the inlargement of his own kingdom, by the eternall destruction of man in the life to come' (James Mason, *The Anatomie of Sorcerie* (1612), p. 55).

42 *Solamen . . . doloris*] Chaucer expresses the same (fairly common-

place) notion in *Troilus and Criseyde*: 'Men seyn, "to wrecche is consola-
cioun To have an-other felawe in his peyne" ' (i. 708–9).

58 propitious] The blasphemy of Faustus's action is emphasized by his
language: Christ's blood was shed to be propitious for the sins of mankind, and Christians are reminded of this in the 'comfortable words' of
the Book of Common Prayer, spoken before the celebration of Holy
Communion: 'If any man sin, we have an Advocate with the Father,
Jesus Christ the righteous; and He is the propitiation for our sins' (I John
2: 1).

71 cleare] Greg observes that no earthly fire will liquefy congealed
blood.

74 *Consummatum est*] 'It is finished'; the last words of Christ on the
cross (St John 19: 30).

77 *Homo fuge*] 'Fly, O man.'

97 a spirit in forme and substance] The interpretation of this first
clause is crucial for an understanding of subsequent developments in the
play. Thomas Nashe, although no theologian, can provide some helpful
information about diabolic nature and power. In *Pierce Penilesse His
Supplication to the Divell* the question is asked 'whether there are . . .
good Spirits as well as evill?' It is answered categorically: 'Naie, certeinlie
(quoth he) we are all evill'. The answer is then expounded a little:

whereas the Diuines attribute unto us these good and evill spirits, the
good to guide us from evil, and the evill to draw us from goodnesse, they
are not called spirits, but Angels, of which sort was *Raphaell*, the good
Angell of *Tobias*, who exilde the evill spirit *Asmodius* into the desart of
Aegypt.

The questioner persists, demanding to know whether the devils 'have
power to hurt granted them from God or from themselves'? He is told:

although that divels be most mightie spirites, yet can they not hurt but
permissively, or by some speciall dispensation: as when a man is fallen
into the state of an out-law, the Law dispenseth with them that kill him,
& the Prince excludes him from the protection of a subject, so, when a
man is a relaps from GOD and his Lawes, God withdrawes his prouid-
ence from watching ouer him, and authoriseth the deuil, as his instrument, to assault and torment him . . . (McKerrow, i. 235–6)

According to some theologians (who followed Aquinas), God could
have no mercy on the devils, who were *ipso facto* incapable of repenting;
John Donne explained:

To those that fall, can appertain no reconciliation: no more then to those
that die in their sins; for *Quod homini mors, Angelis casus*: The fall of the

Angels wrought upon them, as the death of a man does upon him. (Sermon 11 in *The Sermons of John Donne*, ed. G. R. Potter and E. M. Simpson (1959), iv. 299).

Cf. also W. W. Greg, 'The Damnation of Faustus', *Modern Language Review*, xli (1946), 97–107; Helen Gardner, 'The Theme of Damnation in *Dr Faustus*', in *'Dr Faustus': A Casebook*, ed. John Jump (1969), pp. 95–100; and Roma Gill, 'The Christian Ideology of *Dr Faustus*', in *Théâtre et Idéologies* ed. M. T. Jones-Davies (Paris, 1982), pp. 179–200.

122 these elements] The four elements (fire, air, earth, and water) below the sphere of the moon.

128 purified] All created beings ('creatures') are, like the earth, composed of the four elements that go to make up the sublunar world; at the end of the world these mixed creatures will be refined into a pure substance.

141–53 How . . . whore] The writing here seems to degenerate as the text is used simply to introduce some stage business with the devil-wife; the careless '&c' is probably to be spoken by the actor (*etcetera*) rather than the kind of licence given at scene 8 line 11. The B text makes an effort to tidy the lines:

Nay, and this be hell, I'le willingly be damn'd.
What sleeping, eating, walking and disputing?
But leaving this, let me have a wife, the fairest Maid in *Germany*, for I
am wanton and lascivious, and cannot live without a wife.
MEPH. Well *Faustus*, thou shalt have a wife.
    He fetches in a woman devill.
FAUST. What sight is this?
MEPH. Now *Faustus* wilt thou have a wife?
FAUST. Here's a hot whore indeed; no, I'le no wife.

142 disputing] For Faustus, 'disputing' is a function as natural and normal as 'walking'; moreover, it is his 'sweete delight', as the Prologue observes (line 18).

159 *Penelope*] The wife of Ulysses, who remained faithful to her husband during his absence at the Trojan War and for the ten years of his subsequent voyaging (the subject of Homer's *Odyssey*).

160 *Saba*] The Queen of Sheba, who confronted Solomon with 'hard questions' (I Kings 10).

169 Thankes *Mephastophilus*] B allows no investigation of the magic book, ending the episode abruptly with Faustus's thanks:

Thankes *Mephastophilis* for this sweete booke.
This will I keepe, as chary as my life.   *Exeunt.*

The departure of the two characters is followed by the entrance of Wagner with the choric speech that prefaces the arrival in Rome; then the scene continues as in the A text.

175 dispositions] In astrology, the 'disposition' of a planet refers to its relationship with other planets.

182 SD In the B text, Faustus leaves the stage after the episode with the magic book (which is somewhat curtailed). The choric speech introducing the papal banquet (Chorus 2) is inserted, followed by the stage direction '*Enter* FAUSTUS *in his Study, and* MEPHOSTOPHILIS'. The two texts continue more or less in parallel for the episode of the Seven Deadly Sins.

186 Why *Faustus*] B offers a whole line:' 'Twas thine own seeking *Faustus*, thanke thy selfe.'

195 a spirite] See *note* to line 97.

200 My hearts so hardned] Hardness of heart is recognized as a very complex spiritual condition; the Litany of the Book of Common Prayer of the Church of England prays 'From all blindness of heart . . . Good Lord, deliver us.' Some idea of the difficulty of Faustus's position may be appreciated from the following section of the *Summa Theologiae* of St Thomas Aquinas:

In this context darkening of the mind and hardening of the heart have a twofold origin. On the one hand the human soul actively clings to evil and turns away from God's enlightenment. From this point of view God cannot darken the mind or harden the heart just as he cannot cause sin.

On the other hand, however, this also comes from the withholding of grace which would otherwise provide divine illumination so that the mind would view things rightly and the heart would respond tenderly to what was right. And from this point of view God is the cause of spiritual blindness and hardness of heart . . .

By his own choice, however, God withholds the light of grace from those in whom he finds an obstacle. In this case grace is absent not only because man has set an obstacle in its way but because God of his own accord has not set it before man. (*Summa Theologiae*, ed. Thomas Gilby (London and New York, 1964–81), xxv. 212–15).

Cf. also John Donne, Holy Sonnet 2 (*The Divine Poems*, ed. Helen Gardner (1952)):

> Yet grace, if thou repent, thou canst not lacke;
> But who shall give thee that grace to begin?

203–4 swordes . . . steele] In *A Looking Glass for London* by Thomas Lodge and Robert Greene (1594) the Usurer is tempted to suicide by a proferred knife and rope.

208 blinde *Homer*] Homer was traditionally held to be blind.

209 *Alexanders* love ... death] Alexander, son of Priam, is better known as Paris, the lover of Helen of Troy. Before he met Helen, however, Paris was married to Oenone, a nymph of Mount Ida who had the gift of prophecy, as well as certain healing powers. She foretold her husband's desertion and the fall of Troy; she also prophesied that he would return to seek her medical skill in the hour of his death. Paris/Alexander was wounded when the Greeks fought against Troy, and he returned, only to die in Oenone's arms. Oenone bathed his body with her tears, and then stabbed herself. The story of Oenone's love is told by Ovid in *Heroides* V.

210 he ... *Thebes*] The myth is told of Amphion, son of Jupiter; in his Commentary on Ovid's *Metamorphosis* (1632), George Sandys recounts and explains that Amphion was said 'to have drawn the stones together, and built it with the musicke of his harpe; in that by his wisdome and eloquence he brought the savage people to civility, and caused them to cohabit'. Cf. the anonymous *The Taming of A Shrew*, III. vi. 31–2: 'As once did Orpheus with his harmony | And ravishing sound of his melodious harp'.

216 Astrologie] In *EFB* (ch. 18) a confused Faustus asks Mephostophiles for clarification: 'when I conferre Astronomia and Astrologica, as the Mathematicians and auncient writers have left in memory, I finde them to vary and very much to disagree: wherefore I pray thee to teach me the truth in this matter.' The Faustus of Marlowe's source was an astrologer—a calendar-maker and weather-forecaster—rather than an astronomer, and although Mephostophiles promises to teach him about the planets, the approach is unscientific and the information a miscellaneous jumble. Marlowe's protagonist has the questioning mind of the Renaissance student, and the answers he is given accord fairly well with sceptical authorities of the day. See Paul H. Kocher, *Christopher Marlowe* (Chapel Hill, NC, 1946), pp. 214–23, and F. R. Johnson, 'Marlowe's Astronomy and Renaissance Skepticism', *English Literary History* xiii (4) (1946). The Ptolemaic system, as yet unshaken by Copernicus, held that the universe was composed of concentric spheres, with the earth (*this centricke earth*) as the innermost. Beyond the earth was the sphere of the Moon, and further out still the spheres of the six other planets: Mercury, Venus, Sun, Mars, Jupiter, Saturn. The eighth was the firmament, or sphere of the fixed stars, which Marlowe, admitting only nine spheres (line 241), identified with the *Primum Mobile*, the first moving thing which imparted movement to all the rest. The ninth sphere (tenth, if the *Primum Mobile* was allowed to be separate from the firmament) was the immovable empyrean ('the imperiall heaven').

217–223 Tel me . . . pole] Faustus asks first for confirmation of the number of spheres beyond the Moon and whether in fact these do form a single ball. He is told that just as the four elements enclose each other (earth is surrounded by water, water by air, and air by fire), so each sphere or heaven is circled round by the ones beyond it, and all rotate upon a single axletree.

224–5 Nor . . . starres] Saturn, Mars, Jupiter, and the other planets are individually recognizable, and are called *erring* or wandering stars to distinguish them from the fixed stars joined to the firmament. It is quite correct (says Mephastophilis) to give the names of pagan gods to planets: 'in medieval and Renaissance thought the mythic and planetary entities were merged, the personalities of the gods becoming the astrological attributes of their respective planets' (Ormerod and Wortham). Cf. Jean Seznec, *The Survival of the Pagan Gods* (Princeton, NJ, 1953).

226–37 all . . . dayes] 'Do all the planets move at the same speed and in the same direction?' is Faustus's next question. He is told that the planets have two movements: a daily east to west rotation round the earth governed by the *Primum Mobile*, and a slower, individual turning from west to east. Caxton (*Mirrour of the World* (1480), i. 13) explains that each planet is like a fly crawling on a wheel; if the fly crawls in one direction and the wheel turns in the opposite, the fly may be said to have two movements. Faustus knows this well enough, and proceeds to detail with reasonable accuracy the different times taken by the planets in their individual revolutions. The farthest from the earth naturally takes the longest. The figures usually given are: Saturn 29½ years; Jupiter 11¾ years; Mars 1 year 11 months; Sun 1 year; Venus 7½ months; and Mercury 3 months.

237 fresh mens suppositions] Elementary facts given to first-year undergraduates as the basis for an argument.

238 hath every . . . *Intelligentij*] This question relates to a theory first propounded by Plato and developed in the Middle Ages, that each planet was guided by an angelic spirit, commonly called the *intelligence*:

> Let mans Soule be a Sphaere, and then, in this,
> The intelligence that moves, devotion is.

(John Donne, 'Good Friday, Riding Westwards', *The Divine Poems*, ed. Helen Gardner (1952))

Mephastophilis affirms the *Intelligentij*, but the theory was never seriously entertained by scientists.

241–2 Nine . . . heaven] Milton describes a similar cosmology in *Paradise Lost*, when he identifies 'the planets seven', 'the fixed', 'And that crystalline sphere . . . that first moved' (II. 481–3). Marlowe's 'imperial heaven' is the same as Milton's *Primum Mobile*.

243–5 why . . . lesse] Faustus asks about the behaviour of the planets, using technical but well-known astronomical terms: *conjunctions* are the apparent joinings together of two planets, while *oppositions* describes their relationships when most remote:

> Therefore the love which us doth bind,
> But Fate so enviously debars,
> Is the Conjunction of the Mind,
> And Opposition of the Stars.

(Marvell, 'The Definition of Love' (*Complete Poetry*, ed. George de Lord (1968))

Any position between the two extremes of *conjunction* and *opposition* is termed an *aspect*. To astrologers the differing situations and relations of the planets all have some particular significance—hence the horoscope. Faustus is finally told what he already knows: that the heavenly bodies do not all move at the same speed, and that for this reason ('Through an irregular motion so far as the whole is concerned') there are more eclipses etc. in some years than in others. The answer given by Mephastophilis sounds like a quotation from some academic treatise.

255 against our kingdom] Cf. *EFB*: 'I am not bound unto thee in such respects as concerne the hurt of our Kingdome' (ch. 19).

268 have intrest in] Have a legal claim on.

278–80 Never . . . downe] These lines are omitted in the B text.

282 to shew thee some pastime] In *EFB* Lucifer tells Faustus 'I am come to visite thee and to shewe thee some of our hellish pastimes, in hope that will drawe and confirme thy minde a little more stedfast unto us' (ch. 19). The 'pastime' is the appearance, in animal form, of seven major devils. Boas suggests that Richard Tarlton's play *The Seven Dead-lie Sins* (performed by Strange's Men on 6 March 1592) might have provided the idea—and the costumes—for *Dr Faustus*.

287 this shew] Shows were to be distinguished from plays, as Nashe remarked in *Summer's Last Will and Testament*, describing an entertainment which was a mixture of songs, speeches, and dancing: 'nay, 'tis no Play neyther, but a shewe' (McKerrow, iii. 235).

289 to end of scene. This episode has been expanded, and the various appearances rearranged, in the B text.

293 *Ovids* flea] The song *Carmen de Pulice* was popularly attributed to Ovid, although it is probably medieval in origin. In it the poet envies the flea for its freedom of movement over his mistress's body. Cf. N. E.

Lemaire, *Poetae Latini Minores* (Paris, 1826): '*Is quocumque placet, nil tibi, saeve, latet*'.

297 cloth of arras] Tapestry woven at Arras, in Flanders, was used for wall-hangings.

301 churle . . . bag] The specific sense of *churl* = miser is *OED* 6; the 'bag' is his purse.

309 this case of rapiers] A pair of rapiers.

313–14 begotten . . . Oyster wife] Envy is filthy, and stinks.

323 beavers] snacks; drinks or light meals taken between dinner and supper.

327 *Martlemas-biefe*] Meat, salted to preserve it for winter, was hung up around Martinmas (11 November).

320 *March-beere*] A rich ale, made in March and left to mature for a couple of years before drinking.

331 progeny] lineage (the sense is obsolete: *OED* 5).

343–4 inch . . . stock fish] Lechery prefers a small quantity of virility to a large extent of impotence; for the obscene use of 'stock fish' (dried cod) cf. *Measure for Measure*, III. ii. 108: 'he was begot between two stock-fishes'.

344 first letter] Cf. Thomas Middleton, *The Family of Love* (?1604), II. iii, 'Her name begins with Mistress Purge.'

346 Away . . . hel] B provides for a 'piper' here, and assigns the speech to Lucifer (A is unspecific; Ormerod and Wortham offer the line to Faustus).

350–52 O might . . . midnight] Cf. *EFB* (ch. 20): 'Quoth Faustus, I would know of thee if I may see Hell and take a view thereof? That thou shalt (said the divell) and at midnight I will fetch thee.'

353 take this booke] Cf. *EFB* (ch. 20): 'Lucifer . . . gave Faustus a booke, saying, holde, doe what thou wilt, which hee looking upon, straightwaies changed himselfe into a Hog, then into a Worme, then into a Dragon.'

Scene 6

In the A text the two episodes with Robin and Rafe are presented as a single scene, which follows the Chorus (here numbered 'Chorus 3') intro-ducing the scene at the imperial court. In the present edition the scene is divided, and the two episodes positioned, as in B (the second scene is here scene 8); but the local textual variants are so numerous as to demand a separate printing for the B scenes in Appendix B (p. 109). Neither of the characters Robin and Rafe can be identified with the Clown who jested with Wagner in scene 4. The comic style is very different—although equally formulaic.

23 ipocrase] Hippocras was a spiced wine.

23 taberne] A2 has 'modernized' its spelling to 'Taverne'.

Chorus 2

In the B text this speech is inserted, quite inappropriately, after the magic book episode (scene 5), and then repeated in the present position with some additions. Much of the material for this scene is found in *EFB* (ch. 22).

0 SD *Enter* WAGNER] This direction is enough to suggest that all the choric speeches (including the Prologue and the Epilogue) were spoken by Wagner, either *in propria persona* or with some kind of disguise.

4 *Olympus*] Mount Olympus was the home of the gods in Greek mythology.

6 yoked] George Chapman uses the word 'yokie' (*Iliad* (*c*.1611), xvii, line 382: 'the yokie sphere'), but this is scarcely enought to justify A's reading against the common sense of B's emendation. The B text goes on to add, after A's line 6:

> He viewes the cloudes, the Planets, and the Starres,
> The Tropick, Zones, and quarters of the skye,
> From the bright circle of the horned Moone,
> Even to the height of *Primum Mobile*:
> And whirling round with this circumference,
> From East to West his Dragons swiftly glide,
> And in eight daies did bring him home againe.
> Not long he stayed within his quiet house,
> But new exploits do hale him out agen,
> And mounted then upon a Dragons backe,
> That with his wings did part the subtle aire.

7 *Cosmography*] B adds a line of explanation: 'That measures costs, and kingdomes of the earth'.

10 *Peters* feast] St Peter's feast day is 29 June.

Scene 7

Most of the 'guidebook' details are taken from *EFB* (Appendix A, ch. 22).

2 *Trier*] Treves, in West Germany; in the sixteenth century it was important as an administrative, commercial, and cultural centre.

7 river *Maine*] The river is in West Germany.

8 Whose . . . vines] A detail not present in *EFB*.

9 *Naples . . . Campania*] Naples lies within the region of Campania.

13 learned *Maroes*] The poet Virgil (Publius Virgilius Maro) was buried in Naples in 19 BC, and posthumously acquired some reputation as a magician. His tomb stands at the end of the promontory of Posilippo between Naples and Pozzuoli, and legend ascribes the tunnel through this promontory to his magic art.

16 and the rest] B tries to be more precise with 'to the East'—but the direction is not clear.

17 In midst of which] Again, B tries to clarify; but only emphasizes A's vagueness.
a sumptuous Temple] St Mark's Church in Venice; but unless the nearby campanile is intended, the *aspiring toppe* exists only in the dramatist's imagination. The B text, having recourse to *EFB*, adds further details of the church:

> Whose frame is paved with sundry coloured stones,
> And roof't aloft with curious worke in gold.

22 within the walles of Rome] Among the properties belonging to the Admiral's Men in 1598 was 'The sittie of Rome'—perhaps some kind of backcloth for a scene like this (Henslowe, p. 319).

23–87 Faustus I have . . .] From this point the A and B texts are only incidentally similar; see Appendix B, p. 110, for B's version. Variants noted here—or in collation—are remarked only when there is difficulty in A.

33–4 Just . . . parts] Presumably B's editor noticed a surprising deficiency in A (the 'foure stately bridges' must 'leane' over *something*); the information about the Tiber could be found in *EFB*.

37 *Ponto Angelo*] The Pons Aelius was built in AD 35 by Hadrian to connect his mausoleum with the Campus Martius. The mausoleum (directly facing the bridge, not standing on it) became the Castello di S. Angelo.

40–41 And . . . yeare] B expands and explains the line:

> As that the double Cannons forg'd of brasse,
> Do watch [?match] the number of the daies contain'd,
> Within the compasse of one compleat yeare.

42 piramides] The obelisk that stands in front of St Peter's was brought to Rome from Egyptian Thebes by Caligula in the first century AD. The plural form *piramides* is often used as a singular—and here gives the additional syllable demanded for a regular pentameter.

45–6 *Styx . . . Phlegiton*] Rivers of Hades, the Greek underworld; in *Paradise Lost* Milton describes:

> Abhorred Styx the flood of deadly hate,
> Sad Acheron of sorrow, black and deep;
> Cocytus, named of lamentation loud
> Heard on the rueful stream; fierce Phlegethon
> Whose waves of torrent fire inflame with rage.   (ii. 577–81)

48 scituation] *OED* lists this as a variant spelling for *situation*; the word here (and in *EFB*) seems to mean 'lay-out' rather than the usual 'location'. Greg quotes a similar usage in Samuel Rowley's *When You See Me You Know Me* (1605):

> Meane while, your Maiesty may heere behold
> This warlike kingdome[s] faire *Metropolis*,
> The Citty *London*, and the river *Thames*,
> And note the scituation of the place.

53 *summum bonum*] A term used in scholastic theology to denote the nature of God.

59 SD CARDINALL of Lorraine] The identity of the Pope's guest varies: in *EFB* (ch. 22) it is the Cardinal of Pavia who is entertained; the B text has the Archbishop of Rheims.

61 the divel choake you] Greg suggested that this repetition of Gluttony's phrase (scene 5 line 334) could indicate common authorship for the present section and the episode with the Seven Deadly Sins.

74 pardon] A papal indulgence (*OED pardon* 3a).

75 dirge] The word derives from the antiphon (*Dirige Domine Deus . . .*) at Matins in the Office for the Dead; it was used as a name for that service, and by extension for a requiem mass. The term is used properly here by the Pope; but the ritual performed is in fact not a mass but a formal cursing (or commination).

76 SD *The* POPE *crosseth himselfe*] *EFB* describes how the Pope 'would ever be blessing and crossing over his mouth'; see Appendix A (ch. 22).

83 bell, booke, and candle] At the close of the office of excommunication the bell is tolled, the Bible is closed, and the candle extinguished.

90 SD *Sing this*] The two texts converge again.

96 *Sandelo*] Presumably suggested by the friar's sandals.

Scene 8

The many variations in the B text make collation of this scene pointless; for the B scene, see Appendix B, p. 116.

2 *ecce signum*] 'Behold the proof'; a catchword fairly frequent among Elizabethan comic actors—cf. *1 Henry IV*, II. iv. 168, where Falstaff shows his 'sword hack'd like a handsaw—*ecce signum*'.

2–3 heeres a simple purchase] This is clear profit.

11 but a &c] An indication for the actor to 'fribble out the rest' (see Introduction, p. xxi).

27 *O nomine Domine*] This, and the other dog-Latin exclamations, are attempts by the clowns to protect themselves from the devil; cf. *A Looking Glass for London*, line 1698: 'Nominus patrus, I bless me from thee.'

31 SD *Enter to them*] This direction leads Boas and Jump to assume two alternative endings to the scene—but this seems unnecessary. It would be in proper medieval tradition for Mephastophilis to carry off the Vintner; he could then return to cope with Robin and Rafe (who, after all, are the real offenders).

50 out of the potage pot] A near-proverbial expression; cf. Francis Merbury, *Marriage Between Wit and Wisdom* (*c*.1571): 'The cook is not so sone gone as the doges hed is in the porig pot.'

Chorus 3

The B text has no trace of this Chorus, which is obviously intended to move the play's action to the imperial court—just as Chorus 2 relocated the scene at the papal court. In A the Chorus is misplaced, being followed by the two clownage scenes at the inn.

4 beare] The usual form for the past tense of *bear*; *bore* is rare before *c*.1600.

14 *Carolus* the fift] Charles V (1519–56), whose court was at Innsbruck; the earlier part of his reign would have coincided with the life of the historical Faustus.

15 mongst] *OED* cites this as one of the earliest incidences of the aphetic form of *amongst*; the full form is used in A2 and 3.

Scene 9

The source material for this scene is printed in Appendix A (chs 29–30); and B's much expanded version appears in Appendix B, pp. 118–26.

25 *Alexander* the great] Alexander III of Macedon (356–323 BC).

26 preheminence] *OED* recognizes this as a variant spelling for *pre-eminence*; for the sense 'pre-eminent men' cf. the two uses of 'nobility'.

29 motion] Boas thinks this should be 'mention', since *EFB* has the phrase 'as the Chronicles make mention' in the corresponding passage. But Greg suggests that the words 'motion' and 'mention' might be almost synonymous in *OED*'s *motion* 7.

34 Paramour] Probably Roxana, Alexander's wife.

59 *Acteon*] As a punishment for coming upon Diana and her nymphs bathing, Actaeon was turned into a stag, and his own hounds tore him to pieces (Ovid, *Metamorphoses*, III).

74–5 batcheler . . . wife . . . hornes] The old joke that horns were the sign of a cuckolded husband.

78 Bred . . . rocke] Cf. *2 Tamburlaine*, III. ii. 89: 'Fenc'd with the concave of some monstrous rock'.

81 no haste but good] Tilley (H. 199): 'No haste but good (speed)'.

97 thred of vitall life] The image of the thread of life derives from the Greek myth of the three Fates: Clotho spun the thread of human life, which was measured by Lachesis; and Atropos cut it at death.

98 payment] The idea of death as a debt to nature is a commonplace (cf. *Macbeth*, V. ix. 5: 'Your son, my lord, has paid a soldier's debt'); but it is revitalized by Faustus's predicament.

Scene 10

The first Horse-courser episode has been so altered in the B text as to make collation impossible; see Appendix B, p. 126. The *EFB* material is printed in Appendix A (ch. 34).

16 ride him not into the water] Water will dissolve a witch's spell.

17 drinke of all waters] Go anywhere; cf. *Twelfth Night*, IV. ii. 63: 'Nay, I am for all waters'.

22 for fortie] For any large sum of money.

22–3 qualitie of hey ding, ding] The horse-courser seems to be wishing that his horse were a stallion and not a gelding; the phrase calls for an obscene gesture. Cf. Nashe, *Have With You to Saffron Walden* (1596): 'Yea, Madam *Gabriele*, are you such an old ierker! then Hey ding a ding, vp with your petticoate, haue at your plum-tree' (McKerrow, iii. 113).

26 bring his water] i.e. his urine (for diagnosis).

31–5 Thy fatall . . . conceit] The texts coincide for these five lines; they diverge with the reappearance of the Horse-courser.

37 Doctor *Lopus*] Roderigo Lopez, a Spanish Jew, was Queen Eliza-

beth's personal physician; he was executed in February 1594 for his supposed part in a plot to poison her.

45 bottle of hey] Jump quotes Dryden's play, *An Evening's Love*, III. i: 'A witch's horse, you know, when he enters into water, returns into a bottle [= truss] of hay againe'.

48–9 hey, passe] A juggler's catchphrase, used by Nashe ('heathen heigh passe') in *The Unfortunate Traveller* (1594) to denote fantastic behaviour and those who performed it (McKerrow, ii. 259).

56 glasse-windowes] Boas thinks that Faustus 'is apparently supposed to be sitting just behind the windows of his house', but I much prefer Greg's suggestion of 'spectacles'—although no parallel usage has been found.

80 SD *Enter* WAGNER] The two texts coincide again; presumably Faustus is coming towards his own house, and Wagner comes to meet him.

82 Vanholt] *EFB* (ch. 39) has 'Anholt' or 'Anhalt'.

Scene 11

In the B text this scene (which is greatly altered) is preceded by an interlude in which the Clowns narrate some of the Doctor's trickeries. The Clowns reappear at the end of the Vanholt episode. See Appendix A (ch. 39) for the source material, and Appendix B, p. 128, for the B text additions.

0 SD *Enter to them*] On the printed page, this seems like an awkward way of linking two episodes; but in stage terms there is no problem. At the end of scene 9 the action moved, without hindrance, from the imperial court to the 'faire and pleasant greene' where the Horse-courser encountered Faustus; so now the movement is equally smooth as the characters relocate themselves in the banqueting-hall (or some such chamber) belonging to the Duke of Vanholt.

21 twoo circles] This rather confusing explanation is taken from *EFB* (see p. 103).

24 *Saba*] In present-day terms, this is the Yemen.

Scene 12

The A and B versions of this scene are closely related—but B is markedly inferior to A, and in fact reads like a poor memorial reconstruction in the Scholars' part; the Old Man's speech is completely rewritten. The texts come together at line 47. See Appendix B, p. 132. Both texts rely quite heavily on *EFB*; cf. Appendix A (chs 45, 48, 49).

3 *Helen* of *Greece*] The daughter of Leda and Jupiter, Helen was married to Menelaus, King of Sparta, when Paris claimed her as his reward for adjudicating between three goddesses. He carried her off to Troy; and the abduction was the cause of the Trojan War.

13 sir *Paris*] The courtly title seems to transform Paris, son of Priam, into a knight of medieval romance.

14 *Dardania*] In fact, this was the city built by Dardanus on the Hellespont; but the name is often transferred to Troy.

15 danger is in words] Faustus stresses the same need for silence when, in the B text, he prepares the Emperor for the apparitions of Alexander and his paramour: 'demand no questions of the King, But in dumbe silence let them come and goe' (scene 9).

15 SD *passeth over the Stage*] According to Allardyce Nicoll ('Passing over the Stage', *Shakespeare Survey*, xii (1959), 47–55), this directed a movement from the yard, across the stage, and out at the other side of the yard.

21–2 pride . . . excellence] *A Looking Glass for London* uses both these phrases of encomium: 'pride of nature's excellence' (line 433) and 'paragon of excellence' (line 1521).

27–37 To guide . . . guilt] The writing of this speech seems oddly strained: a 'gole' cannot 'conduct', and 'comiseration' does not 'expel'. The speech must have been rewritten for the B text, where it is rather more satisfactory (although, of course, no more efficacious). In function, the Old Man's speech is comparable to the meditation of Mercy in the morality play *Mankind*:

> Without rude behaviour I cannot express this inconvenience.
> Weeping, sighing, and sobbing were my sufficience;
> All inward nutriment to me as carrion is odible;
> My inward affliction yieldeth me tedious unto your presence.
> I cannot bear it evenly that Mankind is so flexible.

(lines 736–40; *Three Late Medieval Morality Plays*, ed. G. A. Lester (London, 1981))

41 SD *gives him a dagger*] In *A Looking Glass for London* the Evil Angel tempts the despairing Usurer by offering a knife and rope. For the dagger as an emblem of despair see also Spenser's *The Faerie Queene*, I. ix. 29 and 51.

62 And with my blood] *EFB* (ch. 49) gives the full text for a second 'deed', written seventeen years after the first.

81–2 Was this . . . *Ilium*] Cf. *2 Tamburlaine*, II. iv. 87–8:

> *Hellen*, whose beauty summoned *Greece* to armes,
> And drew a thousand ships to *Tenedos*.

Troy was called 'Ilium' after its founder Ilos, son of Dardanus.

83 Sweete . . . kisse] Cf. *Dido Queene of Carthage*, IV. iv. 122–3:

> For in his lookes I see eternitie,
> And heele make me immortall with a kisse.

In 'The Expiration' John Donne speaks of a kiss which 'sucks two soules, and vapors both away'; Donne's editor, Helen Gardner, quotes one of the poet's sermons for a serious application of the conceit to the kiss of religious love: 'As in death there is a transmigration of the soule, so in this spiritual love, by this kisse, there is a transfusion of the soule too' (John Donne, *The Songs and Sonnets*, ed. Helen Gardner (Oxford, 1965)).

87 SD *Enter* OLD MAN] B omits this appearance of the Old Man, and his speech at 101–9.

92 *Achillis* . . . heel] The greatest of the Greek warriors in the war against Troy was Achilles; he was invulnerable except in one heel— where he was shot by Paris.

96–7 flaming . . . *Semele*] The sight of Jupiter in all his divine splendour was too much for human eyes, and Semele was consumed by the fire of his brightness.

99 wanton *Arethusaes* azurde armes] Arethusa was a nymph of Elis who bathed in the river Alpheus, thereby exciting the passion of the river-god; it was said by Sandys in his Commentary on *Metamorphosis* V that the god 'drewe his pedegree from the sun'. Alpheus pursued Arethusa until the nymph was changed into a fountain.

104 sift] Cf. St Luke 22: 31: 'Satan hath desired to have you, that he may sift you as wheat.'

Scene 13

B opens this scene with the appearance of Lucifer, Belzebub, and Mephostophilis as spectators of Faustus's end, 'To marke him how he doth demeane himselfe'. See Appendix B, p. 133. For the source material, see Appendix A.

31 drawes in my teares] 'No not so much as their eyes are able to shed teares (thretten and torture them as ye please) while first they repent (God not permitting them to dissemble their obstinacie in so horrible a crime)', James VI and I, *Daemonologie* (Edinburgh, 1597), p. 81.

60 farewel] In the B text this scene continues with a confrontation between Faustus and Mephostophilis, followed by visions of heaven (a

celestial throne) and hell (an infernal kitchen) which are described by the Good and Evil Angels, who part from Faustus with the words (respectively):

> And now poore soule must thy good Angell leave thee,
> The jawes of hell are open to receive thee;

and

> And so I leave thee *Faustus* till anon,
> Then wilt thou tumble in confusion.

61–117 Ah *Faustus* . . . ah *Mephastophilis*] In the B text this final soliloquy has been heavily censored to avoid giving offence after the 1606 Act of Abuses; see Appendix B, p. 137.

64–72 Stand still . . . damnd] Cf. *Edward II*, V. i. 64–70:

> Continue ever thou celestiall sunne,
> Let never silent night possesse this clime,
> Stand still you watches of the element,
> All times and seasons rest you at a stay,
> That *Edward* may be still faire Englands king:
> But dayes bright beames dooth vanish fast away,
> And needes I must resigne my wished crowne.

70 *O lente . . . equi*] The final, and most famous, irony in the play. The line is from Ovid's *Amores*, I. xiii. 40, where the poet wishes for neverending night in the arms of his mistress; in Marlowe's own translation, 'stay night, and runne not thus', the horses were sacrificed to the exigencies of the couplet.

73 leape up . . . pulles me down] Ormerod and Wortham relate this line to the emblem on the title-page of the 1604 edition of the play. A similar device can be found in Geoffrey Whitney's collection, *A Choice of Emblemes* (1586), p. 152.

74 streames in the firmament] T. S. Eliot (in 'Christopher Marlowe', *Selected Essays* (1932)), calls this 'a triumphantly successful remodelling' of the line from *2 Tamburlaine*: 'And set blacke streamers in the firmament' (V. iii. 49).

81–2 Mountaines and hilles . . . God] Cf. Hosea 10: 8: 'And they shall say to the mountains, Cover us; and to the hills, Fall on us'; see also Revelation, 6: 16, and St Luke, 23: 3. In *A Looking Glass for London* the desperate Usurer utters the same cry:

> Hell gapes for me, heaven will not hold my soule,
> You mountaines shroude me from the God of truth . . .
> Cover me hills, and shroude me from the Lord.
>
> (lines 2054–5, 2059)

85 You starres . . . nativitie] Cf. *1 Tamburlaine*, IV. ii. 33: 'Smile Stars that raign'd at my nativity'; and *2 Tamburlaine*, V. iii. 2: 'Fal starres that governe his nativity.'

86 influence] An ethereal fluid streaming from the stars which acted upon the characters and destinies of men; cf. *The Faerie Queene*, I. viii. 42: 'what evill starre On you hath fround, and pourd his influence bad'. *OED influence* 2.

102 *Pythagoras metem su cossis*] Pythagoras of Samos, a philosopher of the sixth century BC, was regarded as the authority for the doctrine of the transmigration of souls, whereby the human soul at the death of the body took on some other form of life. The phonetic spelling of the A text was later, in A3, replaced by the more orthodox 'metemsycosis'.

104 al beasts are happy] Cf. Nashe, *Christs Teares Over Jerusalem* (1593): 'Thrice blessed are Beastes that die soone, and after this life feele no hell' (McKerrow, ii. 113).

117 Ile burne my bookes] All magicians who renounced their art made a solemn act of disposing of their magic books; cf. Prospero in *The Tempest*:

> I'll break my staff,
> Bury it certain fadoms in the earth
> And deeper than did ever plummet sound
> I'll drown my book.   (V. i. 54–7)

117 SD *exeunt with him*] The B text (see Appendix B, p. 138) here inserts a grotesquely macabre scene where the Scholars discover Faustus's body, its 'limbs, All torne asunder by the hand of death'. Both texts conclude, in the homiletic tradition of the morality play, with the Epilogue.

Epilogue

2 *Apolloes* Laurel bough] The laurel wreath of the poet (or Conjuror) laureate; in *Pilgrimage to Parnassus* Consiliodorus gives instructions as he sends his sons

> To Hellicon faire, that pure and happie springe.
> Return triumphant with your laurell boughes,
> With Phoebus trees decke your deservinge brows.   (I. i. 106–8)

Motto *Terminat . . . opus*] 'The hour ends the day; the author ends his work.' It seems likely that this line, of unknown origin, was appended to the play by the printer and not by Marlowe.

APPENDIX A: *THE ENGLISH FAUSTBOOK*

Substantial passages, which form a coherent narrative, are printed in this Appendix. Other details from Marlowe's source are included in the Commentary. Spelling and punctuation follow those of the original text, but the copy's use of italics has been disregarded. The copy used is in the British Library, C.27.6.43.

THE
HISTORIE
of the damnable
life, and deserved death of
Doctor Iohn Faustus,
Newly imprinted, and in conveni-
ent places imperfect matter amended:
according to the true Copie printed
at Franckfort, *and translated into*
English by P.F. *Gent.*

Chapter 1

John Faustus borne in the town of Rhode lying in the Province of Weimer in Germanie his father a poore Husbandman, and not able wel to bring him up: but having an Uncle at Wittenberg, a rich man, and without issue, took this J. Faustus from his father, and made him his heire, in so much that his father was no more troubled with him, for he remained with his Uncle at Wittenberg, where he was kept at the Universities in the same cities to study divinity. But Faustus being of a naughty mind and otherwise addicted, applied not his studies, but tooke himselfe to other exercises ... he gave himselfe secretly to study Necromancy and Conjuration, in so much that few or none could perceive his profession

...

... Faustus continued to study in the University, and was by the Rectors and sixteene Masters afterwards examined howe he had profited in his studies, and being found by them, that none for his time were able to argue with him in Divinity, or for the excellency of his wisedome to compare with him, with one consent they made him Doctor of Divinitie. But Doctor Faustus within short time after hee had obtayned his degree, fell into such fantasies and deepe cogitations, that he was marked of many . . . For he accompanied himselfe with divers that were seene in those divelish Arts, and that had the Chaldean, Persian, Hebrew, Arabian, and Greeke tongues, using Figures, Characters, Conjurations, Incantations, with many other ceremonies belonging to these infernal Arts, as Necromancie, Charmes, Southsaying, Witchcraft, Inchantment, being delighted with their bookes, words, and names so well, that he studied day and night therein: in so much that hee could not abide to bee called Doctor of Divinitie, but waxed a worldly man, and named himselfe an Astrologian and a Mathematician . . .

Chapter 2

You have heard before, that all Faustus minde was set to study the artes of Necromancie and Conjuration, the which exercise hee followed day and night: and taking to him the wings of an Eagle, thought to flie over the whole world, and to know the secrets of heaven and earth; for his Speculation was so wonderfull, being expert in using his Vocabula, Figures, Characters, Conjurations, and other Ceremoniall actions, that in all the haste hee put in practise to bring the Divell before him. And taking his way to a thicke Wood neere to Wittenberge . . . he came into the same wood towards evening into a crosse way, where he made with a wand a Circle in the dust, and within that many more Circles and Characters: and thus he past away the time untill it was nine or ten of the clocke in the night, then began Doctor Faustus to call for Mephostophiles the Spirite, and to charge him in the name of Beelzebub to appeare there personally without any long stay: then presently the Divel began so great a rumor in the Wood as if heaven and earth would have come together . . . Faustus all this while halfe amazed at the Divels so long tarrying, and doubting whether he were best to abide any more such horrible Conjurings, thought to leave his Circle and depart; whereupon the Divel made him such musicke of all sortes, as if the Nimphes themselves had been in place: whereat Faustus was revived and stoode stoutly in his Circle aspecting his purpose, and began againe to conjure the spirite Mephostophiles in the name of the Prince of Devils to appeare in his likenesse . . . where at sodainly over his head hanged hovering in the ayre a mighty Dragon . . . [which] changed it selfe into a Globe . . .

. . . Faustus vexed at the Spirits so long tarying, used his Charmes with full purpose not to depart before he had his intent, and crying on Mephostophiles the Spirit; sodainly the Globe opened and sprang up in

height of a man: so burning a time, in the end it converted to the shape of
a fiery man. This pleasant beast ranne about the circle a great while, and
lastly appeared in manner of a gray Frier, asking Faustus what was his request. Faustus commaunded that the next morning at twelve of the
clocke hee should appeare to him at his house; but the devil would in no
wise graunt: Faustus began againe to conjure him in the name of Beelzebub, that he should fulfil his request: whereupon the Spirit agreed, and
so they departed each one his way.

Chapter 3

Doctor Faustus having commaunded the Spirit to be with him, at his
houre appointed he came and appeared in his chamber, demanding of
Faustus what his desire was: then began Doctor Faustus anew with him
to conjure him that he should be obedient unto him, and to answer him
certain Articles, and to fulfil them in al points.

1 That the Spirit should serve him and be obedient unto him in all
things that he asked of him from that houre until the houre of his death.

2 Farther, any thing he desired of him he should bring it to him.

3 Also, that in all Faustus his demaunde or Interrogations, the spirit
should tell him nothing but that which is true.

Hereupon the Spirit answered and laid his case foorth, that he had no
such power of himselfe, until he had first given his Prince (that was ruler
over him) to understand thereof, and to know if he could obtaine so much
of his Lord: therfore speake farther, that I may do thy whole desire to my
Prince: for it is not in my power to fulfill without his leave. Shew me the
cause why (said Faustus). The Spirit answered; Faustus, thou shalt
understand, that with us it is even as well a kingdome, as with you on
earthe: yea, we have our rulers and servants, as I my selfe am one, and we
name our whole number the Legion: for although that Lucifer is thrust
and fallen out of heaven through his pride and high minde, yet he hath
notwithstanding a Legion of Divels at his commaundement, that we call
the Oriental Princes; for his power is so great and infinite. Also there is an
host in Meridie, in Septentrio, in Occidente: and for that Lucifer hath his
kingdome under heaven, wee must change and give our selves unto men
to serve them at their pleasure. It is also certaine, we have never as yet
opened unto any man the truth of our dwelling, neither of our ruling,
neither what our power is, neither have we given any man any gift, or
learned him any thing, except he promise to be ours.

Doctor Faustus upon this arose where he sate, and said, I wil have my
request, and yet I wil not be damned. The spirit answered, Then shalt
thou want thy desire, and yet art thou mine notwithstanding: if any man
would detaine thee it is in vain, for thine infidelity hath confounded thee.

Chapter 4

Faustus continuing in his divelish cogitations, never moving out of the place where the Spirit left him (such was his fervent love to the divel) the night approaching, this swift flying Spirit appeared to Faustus, offering himself with al submission to his service, with ful authority from his Prince to doe whatsoever he would request, if so be Faustus would promise to be his: this answere I bring thee, and an answere must thou make by me againe, yet will I heare what is thy desire, because thou hast sworne me to be here at this time. Doctor Faustus gave him this answere, though faintly (for his soules sake) That his request was none other but to become a Divel, or at the least a limme of him, and that the Spirit should agree unto these Articles as followeth.

1 That he might be a Spirite in shape and qualitie.

2 That Mephostophiles should be his servant, and at his commande-ment.

3 That Mephostophiles should bring him anything, and doo for him whatsoever.

4 That at all times he should be in his house, invisible to all men, except onely to himself, and at his commandement to shew himselfe.

5 Lastly, that Mephostophiles should at all times appeare at his com-maund, in what forme or shape soever he would.

Upon these poynts the Spirit answered Doctor Faustus, that all this should be granted him and fulfilled, and more if he would agree unto him certaine Articles as followeth.

First, that Doctor Faustus should give himselfe to his Lord Lucifer, body and soule.

Secondly, for confirmation of the same, he should make him a writing, written with his owne blood.

Thirdly, that he would be an enemie to all Christian people.

Fourthly, that he would denie his Christian beliefs.

Fiftly, that he let not any man change his opinion, if so bee any man should goe about to disswade, or withdraw him from it.

Further, the spirit promised Faustus to give him certaine yeares to live in health and pleasure, and when such yeares were expired, that then Faustus should be fetched away, and if he should holde these Articles and conditions, that then he should have all whatsoever his heart would wish or desire; and that Faustus should quickly perceive himself to be a Spirit in all maner of actions whatsoever. Hereupon Doctor Faustus his minde was so inflamed, that he forgot his soule, and promised Mephostophiles to hold all things as hee had mentioned them: he thought the divel was not so black as they use to paynt him, nor hell so hote as the people say, etc.

Chapter 5

. . . After a while, Faustus promised Mephostophiles to write and make his Obligation, with full assurance of the Articles in the Chapter before rehearsed. A pitifull case, (Christian Reader,) for certainly this Letter or Obligation was found in his house after his most lamentable end, with all the rest of his damnable practises used in his whole life. Therefore I wish al Christians to take an example by this wicked Faustus, and to be comforted in Christ, contenting themselves with that vocation whereunto it hath pleased God to call them, and not to esteeme the vaine delights of this life, as did this unhappie Faustus, in giving his Soule to the Divell: and to confirme it the more assuredly, he tooke a small penknife, and prickt a vaine in his left hand, and for certaintie thereupon, were seene on his hand these words written, as if they had been written with blood, O HOMO FUGE; whereat the Spirit vanished, but Faustus continued in his damnable minde, and made his writing as followeth.

Chapter 6

. . . now have I Doctor John Faustus unto the hellish prince of Orient and his messenger Mephostophiles, given both bodie and soule, upon such condition, that they shall learne me, and fulfill my desire in all things, as they have promised and vowed unto me, with due obedience unto me, according unto the Articles mentioned betweene us.

Further, I covenant and grant with them by these presents, that at the end of 24 yeares next ensuing the date of this present Letter, they being expired, and I in the meane time, during the said yeares be served of them at my wil, they accomplishing my desires to the full in al points as we are agreed, that then I give them full power to doe with mee at their pleasure, to rule, to send, to fetch, or carrie me or mine, be it either body, soule, flesh, blood, or goods, into their habitation, be it wheresoever . . .

Chapter 8

. . . Faustus kept a boy with him that was his scholler, an unhappie wagge, called Christopher Wagner, to whome this sporte and life that hee saw his master follow seemed pleasant. Faustus loved the boy well, hoping to make him as good or better seene in his divelish exercise than himselfe . . .

Chapter 9

Doctor Faustus continued thus in his Epicurish life day and night, and beleeved not that there was a God, hell, or divel: he thought that bodie and soule died together, and had quite forgotten Divinitie or the immortalitie of his soule, but stoode in his damnable heresie day and night. And bethinking himselfe of a wife, called Mephostophiles to counsaile; which would in no wise agree: demanding of him if he would breake the covenant made with him, or if hee had forgot it. Hast not thou (quoth Mephostophiles) sworne thy selfe an enemy to God and all creatures. To this I answere thee, thou canst not marry; thou canst not serve two masters, God, and my Prince: for wedlock is a chiefe institution ordained of God ... Therefore Faustus, looke well about thee, and bethinke thyselfe better, and I wish thee to change thy minde: for if thou keepe not what thou hast promised in thy writing, we wil teare thee in peeces ...

... Then Faustus said unto him, I am not able to resist nor bridle my fantasie, I must and will have a wife, and I pray thee give thy consent to it ... Hereupon appeared unto him an ougly Divell, so fearefull and monstrous to beholde, that Faustus durst not looke on him. The Divell said, what wouldst thou have Faustus: how likest thou thy wedding? What minde art thou in now: Faustus answered, he had forgot his promise, desiring him of pardon, and he would talke no more of such things. The divell answered, thou were best so to doe, and so vanished.

After appeared unto him his Frier Mephostophiles with a bel in his hand, and spake to Faustus: It is no jesting with us, holde thou that which thou hast vowed, and wee will perform as wee have promised: and more than that, thou shalt have thy hearts desire of what woman soever thou wilt, bee she alive or dead, and so long as thou wilt, thou shalt keepe her by thee ...

Chapter 10

Doctor Faustus living in all manner of pleasure that his heart could desire, continuing in his amorous drifts, his delicate fare, and costly apparel, called on a time his Mephostophiles to him: which being come brought with him a booke in his hand of all maner of divelish and inchanted artes, the which he gave Faustus saying: hold my Faustus, worke now thy hearts desire: The copie of this inchanting booke was afterward found by his servant Christopher Wagner. Wel (quoth Faustus to his spirit) I have called thee to know what thou canst doe if I have neede of thy help. Then answered Mephostophiles and said, my Lord Faustus, I am a flying spirit: yea, so swift as thought can think, to do whatsoever. Here Faustus said: but how came thy Lord and master Lucifer to have so great a fal from heaven: Mephostophiles answered: My Lord Lucifer was a faire Angell, created of God as immortal, and being placed in the Seraphins, which are above the Cherubins, hee would have presumed unto the Throne of God, with intent to have thrust God out of his seate. Upon this presumption the Lord cast him downe headlong, and where before he was an Angel of light, now dwels hee in darkenes . . .

Chapter 11

The night following, after Faustus his communication had with Mephostophiles, as concerning the fal of Lucifer, Doctor Faustus dreamed that he had seene a part of hell: but in what maner it was, or in what place he knew not: whereupon he was greatly troubled in minde, and called unto him Mephostophiles, I pray thee resolve me in this doubt: what is hell, what substance is it of, in what place stands it, and when was it made: Mephostophiles answered: my Faustus, thou shalt knowe, that before the fall of my Lord Lucifer there was no hell, but even then was hell ordained: it is of no substance, but a confused thing . . . but to bee short with thee Faustus, we know that hell hath neither bottome nor end.

Chapter 13

. . . Doctor Faustus, when he had heard the words of his spirit, began to consider with himselfe, having diverse and sundrie opinions in his head: and very pensively (saying nothing) unto his Spirit, hee went into his chamber, and laid him on his bed, recording the words of Mephostophiles; which so pearced his heart, that hee fell into sighing and great lamentation crying out: alas, ah, wo is me! what have I done? Even so shall it come to passe with me: am not I also a creature of Gods making, bearing his owne Image and similitude, into whom he hath breathed the Spirite of life and immortalitie, unto whome hee hath made all things living subject: but woe is me, mine hautie minde, proud aspyring stomack, and filthie flesh, hath brought my soule into perpetuall damnation; yea, pride hath abused my understanding, in so much that I have forgot my maker, the Spirit of God is departed from mee. I have promised the Divell my Soule: and therefore it is but a folly for me to hope for grace, but it must bee even with mee as with Lucifer, throwne into perpetuall burning fire: ah woe is mee that ever I was borne. In this perplexitie lay this miserable Doctor Faustus, having quite forgot his faith in Christ, never falling to repentance truly, thereby to attaine the grace and holy Spirit of God againe, the which would have been able to have resisted the strong assaults of Sathan: For although hee had made him a promise, yet hee might have remembred throughe true repentance sinners come againe into the favour of God; which faith the faithfull firmely holde, knowing they that kill the bodie, are not able to hurt the soule . . .

Chapter 14

After Doctor Faustus had a while pondered and sorrowed with himselfe of his wretched estate, hee called againe Mephostophiles unto him, commaunding him to tell him the judgement, rule, power, attempts, tyranny and temptation of the Divell, and why he was moved to such kinde of living. [Mephostophiles recounted various diabolic temptations, ending] thou knowest by thy selfe Faustus, how we have dealt with thee. To this answered Faustus, why then thou didst also beguile me. Yea (quoth Mephostophiles) why should not we help thee forwards: for so soone as we saw thy heart, how thou didst despise thy degree taken in Divinitie, and didst study to search and know the secrets of our kingdome; even then did we enter into thee, giving thee divers foule and filthy cogitations, pricking thee forward in thine intent, and perswading thee that thou couldst never attaine to thy desire, untill thou hast the help of some divell: and when thou wast delighted with this, then tooke we roote in thee; and so firmely, that thou gavest thy selfe unto us, both body and soule the which thou (Faustus) canst not denie it: Ah, woe is me miserable Faustus; how have I beene deceived . . .

Chapter 15

Doctor Faustus was ever pondering with himselfe how he might get loose from so damnable an ende as he had given himselfe unto, both of body and soule; but his repentance was like to that of Cain and Judas, he thought his sinnes greater then God could forgive, hereupon rested his minde: he looked up to heaven, but sawe nothing therein: for his heart was so possessed with the Divel, that hee could thinke of nought els but of hell and the paynes thereof . . .

[Mephostophiles gave a graphic account of the torments of the damned, and of hel, 'the everlasting pain, in which is neither hope nor mercy', where 'the damned have neither ende nor time appoynted in the which they may hope to be released'.]

Chapter 16

[Mephostophiles lectured to Faustus, explaining the nature of his sin against God.] This is most true (quoth Faustus) but tell me Mephostophiles, wouldst thou be in my case as I am now? Yea, saith the Spirit (and with that fetcht a great sigh) for yet would I so humble my selfe, that I would winne the favour of God. Then (said Doctor Faustus) it were time enough for me if I amended. True (said Mephostophiles) if it were not for thy great sinnes, which are so odious and detestable in the sight of God, that it is too late for thee, for the wrath of God resteth upon thee . . .

Chapter 17

Doctor Faustus having received deniall of his Spirit, to be resolved any more in such like questions propounded; forgot all good workes, and fell to be a Kalender maker by helpe of his Spirit; and also in short time to be a good Astronomer or Astrologian: he had learned so perfectly of his Spirite the course of the Sunne, Moone, and Starres, that he had the most famous name of all the Mathematicks that lived in his time; as may well appeare by his workes dedicated unto sundry Dukes and Lords: for he did nothing without the advice of his Spirit . . .

Chapter 18

Doctor Faustus falling to practise, and making his Prognostications, he was doubtfull in many poynts: wherefore hee called unto him Mephostophiles his spirit, saying: I finde the ground of this science very difficult to attaine unto: for that when I conferre Astronomia and Astrologica, as the Mathematicians and auncient writers have left in memory, I finde them to vary and very much to disagree: wherefore I pray thee to teach me the truth in this matter. To whome his Spirit answered, Faustus, thou shalt know that the practitioners, or speculators . . . have done nothing of themselves certaine . . . ; it is unpossible for an earthly man to attaine unto the knowledge thereof, without the ayde of some Spirit, or els the special gift of God; for such are the hidden works of God from men: yet doe we Spirits that flie and fleete in all Elements, knowe such, and there is nothing to be done, or by the Heavens pretended, but we know it, except onely the day of Dome. Wherefore (Faustus) learne of me, I will teach thee the course and recourse of [7 planetary signs] the cause of winter and summer, the exaltation and declination of the Sunne, the eclipses of the Moone, the distance and height of the Poles, and every fixed Starre, the nature and operation of the elements, fire, ayre, water, and earth, and all that is contained in them, yea herein there is nothing hidden from me, but onely the fift essence, which once thou hadst Faustus at liberty, but now Faustus thou hast lost it past recovery: wherefore leaving that which will not be againe had, learne now of me to make thunder, lightning, hayle, snow, and raine: the clouds to rent, the earth and craggie rockes to shake and split in sunder, the Seas to swell, and rore, and over-run their markes . . .

Chapter 19

[Faustus became frustrated by the devil's constant refusal to answer his questions, and he reproached Mephostophiles] . . . I have taken thee unto mee as a servant to doe mee service, and thy service will be very deare unto me; yet I cannot have any diligence of thee farther than thou list thy selfe, neither doost thou in any thing as it becommeth thee. The spirit replied, my Faustus, thou knowest that I was never against thy commaundments as yet, but readie to serve and resolve thy questions, although I am not bound unto thee in such respects as concerne the hurt of our kingdome, yet was I alwaies willing to answere thee, and so I am still: therefore my Faustus say on boldly, what is thy will and pleasure? At which words, the spirit stole away the heart of Faustus, who spake in this sorte, Mephostophiles, tell me how and after what sorte God made the world, and all the creatures in them, and why man was made after the Image of God?

The spirit hearing this, answered, Faustus thou knowest that all this is in vaine for thee to aske, I knowe that thou art sory for that thou hast done, but it availeth thee not, for I will teare thee in thousands of peeces, if thou change not thine opinions, and hereat hee vanished away. Whereat Faustus al sorrowful for that he had put forth such a question, fel to weeping and to howling bitterly, not for his sinnes towards God, but for that the Divel was departed from him so sodainely, and in such a rage. And being in this perplexitie, hee was sodainely taken in such an extreame cold, as if he should have frozen in the place where he sate, in which, the greatest Divel in hell appeared unto him, with certaine of his hideous and infernal companie in the most ougliest shapes that it was possible to think upon, and traversing the chamber round about where Faustus sate, Faustus thought to himselfe, now are they come for me though my time bee not come, and that because I have asked such questions of my servant Mephostophiles; at whose cogitations, the chiefest Divel which was his Lord, unto whom he gave his soule, that was Lucifer spake in this sorte: Faustus, I have seene thy thoughtes, which are not as thou hast vowed unto me, by vertue of this letter, and shewed him the Obligation that hee had written with his owne blood, wherefore I am come to visit thee and to shewe thee some of our hellish pastimes, in hope that will drawe and confirme thy minde a little more stedfast unto us. Content quoth Faustus, goe too, let mee see what pastime you can make. At which words, the great Divell in his likenes sate him downe by Faustus commanding the rest of the Divels to appeare in their forme, as if they were in hel . . .

Chapter 20

[Faustus demanded to see a more important devil; Beelzebub appeared, and] asked Faustus his pleasure. Quoth Faustus, I would know of thee if I may see Hell and take a view thereof? That thou shalt (said the divell) and at midnight I will fetch thee . . .

Chapter 22

Doctor Faustus having over-runne fifteen yeers of his appointed time, he tooke upon him a journey, with ful pretence to see the whole world . . . Faustus came thorough many a land and Province; as . . . Italie, Campania, the Kingdome of Naples . . . and came to Treir, for that he chiefly desired to see this towne, and the monuments thereof; but there he saw not many wonders, except one fayre Pallace . . . and also a mighty large Castle that was built of bricke, with three walles and three great trenches, so strong that it was impossible for any princes power to win it . . . from whence he departed to Paris . . . He came from Paris to Mentz, where the river of Mayne fals into the Rhine . . . [and then] to Campania in the Kingdome of Neapolis, in which he saw . . . great and high houses of stone, the streetes fayre and large, and straight foorth from one end of the towne to the other as a line, and al the pavement of the Citie was of brick . . . there saw he the Tombe of Virgil; and the high way that hee cutte through that mighty hill of stone in one night, the whole length of an English mile . . . From thence he came to Venice . . . He wondred not a little at the fayrenes of Saint Markes place, and the sumptuous Church standing therein called Saint Markes; how all the pavement was set with coloured stones, and all the Roode or loft of the Church double gilded over. Leaving this he came to Padua . . .

Well, forward he went to Rome, which lay, and doth yet lie, on the river Tybris, the which devideth the Citie in to parts; over the river are foure great stone bridges, and upon the one bridge called Ponte S. Angelo is the castle of S. Angelo, wherein are so many great cast peeces as there are dayes in a yeare . . . ; the Citie hath eleven gates . . . he saw the Pyramide that Julius Caesar brought out of Africa . . . it is 24 fathom long and at the lower end six fathom foure square, and so forth smaller upwards, on the top is a Crucifixe of beaten golde, the stone standeth on foure Lyone of brasse.

But amongst the rest he was desirous to see the Popes Pallace, and his maner of service at his table, wherefore he and his Spirit made themselves invisible, and came into the Popes Court, and privie chamber where he was . . .

[Faustus was present at a feast honouring the Cardinal of Pavia] . . . and as he sate at meate, the Pope would ever be blessing and crossing over his mouth; Faustus could suffer it no longer, but up with his fist and smote the Pope on the face, and withal he laughed that the whole house might heare him, yet none of them sawe him nor knew where he was: the Pope perswaded his company that it was a damned soule, commanding a Masse presently to be said for his deliverie out of Purgatory, which was done: the Pope sate still at meate, but when the latter messe came in to the Popes boord, Doctor Faustus laid hands thereon saying; this is mine:

and so he took both dish and meate . . . but when the Pope and the rest of his crue perceived they were robbed, and knew not after what sort, they perswaded themselves that it was the damned soule that before had vexed the Pope so, and that smote him on the face, wherefore he sent commandement through al the Citie of Rome, that they should say Masse in every Church, and ring al the bels for to lay the walking Spirit, and to curse him with Bel, Booke, and Candle . . .

[In chapters 24–7 Faustus answers various questions about astronomy and astrology.]

Chapter 29

The Emperour Carolus the fifth of that name was personally with the rest of his Nobles and gentlemen at the towne of Inszbruck where . . . Dr Faustus . . . was invited into the court to meat . . . [The Emperor took Faustus] into the privie chamber, whither being come, he sayd unto him: Faustus, I have heard much of thee, that thou art excellent in the black Arte, and none like thee in mine Empire, for men say that thou hast a familiar Spirit with thee and that thou canst do what thou list: it is therefore (saith the Emperour) my request of thee that thou let me see a proofe of thine experience, and I vowe unto thee by the honour of mine Emperiall Crowne, none evill shall happen unto thee for so dooing. Hereupon Doctor Faustus answered his Majestie, that upon those conditions he was ready in any thing that he could, to doe his highnes commaundement in what service he would appoynt him. Wel, then heare what I shall say (quoth the Emperour.) Being once solitarie in my house, I called to mind mine elders and auncestors, how it was possible for them to attain unto so great a degree of authoritie, yea so high, that wee the successors of that line are never able to come neere. As for example, the great and mighty monarch of the worlde Alexander Magnus, was such a lanterne and spectacle to all his successors (as the Cronicles makes mention) of so great riches, conquering, and subduing so many kingdomes, the which I and those that follow me (I feare) shall never bee able to attaine unto: wherefore Faustus, my hearty desire is that thou wouldst vouchsafe to let me see that Alexander, and his Paramour, the which was praysed to be so fayre, and I pray thee shew me them in such sort that I may see their personages, shape, gesture and apparel, as they used in their life time, and that here before my face; to the ende that I may say I have my long desire fulfilled, and to prayse thee to be a famous man in thine art and experience. Doctor Faustus answered: My most excellent Lord, I am ready to accomplish your request in all things, so farre foorth as I and my Spirit are able to performe: yet your Majestie shall know, that their dead bodies

are not able substantially to be brought before you, but such Spirits as
have seene Alexander and his Paramour alive shall appeare unto you in
manner and forme as they both lived in their most florishing time: and
herewith I hope to please your imperial Majestie. Then Faustus went a
little aside to speake to his Spirit, but he returned againe presently, saying: now if it please your Majesty you shall see them, yet upon this condition that you demaund no question of them, nor speake unto them,
which the Emperour agreed unto. Wherewith Doctor Faustus opened the
privy chamber doore, where presently entred the great and mighty
Emperour Alexander Magnus . . . Shortly after Alexander made humble
reverence and went out againe, and comming to the doore his Paramour
met him, she comming in, she made the Emperour likewise reverence . . .
which the Emperour marking, sayd to himselfe; now have I seene two
persons, which my heart hath long wished to beholde, and sure it cannot
otherwise be, sayd he to himselfe, but that the Spirits have changed
themselves into these formes, and have not deceived me . . . and for that
the Emperour would be the more satisfied in the matter, he thought, I
have heard say, that behind her necke she had a great wart or wenne,
wherefore he tooke Faustus by the hand without any words, and went to
see if it were also to be seene on her or not, but she perceiving that he
came to her bowed downe her neck, where he saw a great wart, and hereupon she vanished, leaving the Emperour and the rest well contented.

Chapter 30

When Doctor Faustus had accomplished the Emperours desire in all
things as he was requested, he went foorth into a gallerie, and leaning
over a rayle to looke into the privie garden, he saw many of the Emperours Courtiers walking and talking together, and casting his eyes now this
way, now that way, he espyed a Knight leaning out at a window of the
great hall; who was fast asleepe (for in those days it was hote) but the person shall bee nameless that slept, for that he was a Knight, although it
was done to a little disgrace of the Gentleman: it pleased Doctor Faustus
through the helpe of his Spirit Mephostophiles to firme upon his head as
hee slept, an huge payre of Harts hornes, and as the Knight awaked
thinking to pul in his head, hee hit his hornes against the glasse that the
panes thereof flew about his eares. Think here how this good Gentleman
was vexed, for he could neither get backward nor forward: which when
the Emperour heard al the courtiers laugh, and came forth to see what
was hapened, the Emperour also when he beheld the Knight with so
fayre a head laughed heartily therat, and was therewithall well pleased: at
last Faustus made him quite of his hornes agayne, but the Knight perceived how they came.

Chapter 34

In like manner hee served an Horse-courser at a faire called Pheiffring, for Doctor Faustus through his cunning had gotten an excellent fayre Horse, whereupon he rid to the Fayre, where hee had many Chap-men that offered him money: lastly, he sold him for 40 Dollers, willing him that bought him, that in anywise he should not ride him over any water, but the Horsecourser marveiled with himself that Faustus bad him ride him over no water, (but quoth he) I will proove, and forthwith hee rid him into the river, presently the horse vanished from under him, and he sate on a bundell of strawe, in so much that the man was almost drowned. The horsecourser knewe well where hee lay that had solde him his horse, wherefore he went angerly to his Inne, where hee found Doctor Faustus fast a sleepe, and snorting on a bed, but the horsecourser could no longer forbeare him, tooke him by the leg and began to pull him off the bed, but he pulled him so, that he pulled his leg from his body, in so much that the Horse-courser fel down backwardes in the place, then began Doctor Faustus to crie with an open throate, he hath murdered me. Hereat the Horse-courser was afraide, and gave the flight, thinking none other with himselfe, but that hee had pulled his leg from his bodie; by this meanes Doctor Faustus kept his money.

Chapter 39

Doctor Faustus on a time came to the Duke of Anholt, the which welcomed him very courteously, this was in the moneth of January, where sitting at the table, he perceived the Dutchesse to be with childe, and . . . said Doctor Faustus to the Dutchesse, Gracious Ladie, I have alway heard, that the great bellied women doe alwaies long for some dainties, I beseech therefore your Grace hide not your mind from me, but tell me what you desire to eate, she answered him, Doctor Faustus now truely I will not hide from you what my heart dooth most desire, namely that if it were now Harvest, I would eate my bellie full of ripe Grapes, and other daintie fruite. Doctor Faustus answered hereupon, Gracious Lady, this is a small thing for me to doe, for I can doe more than this, wherefore he took a plate, and made open one of the casements of the windowe, holding it forth, where incontinent hee had his dish full of all maner of fruites, as red and white Grapes, Peares, and Apples, the which came from out of strange Countries, all these he presented the Dutchesse, saying: Madame, I pray you vouchsafe to taste of this daintie fruite, the which came from a farre Countrey, for ther the Sommer is not yet ended. The Dutchesse thanked Faustus highly, and she fell to her fruite with full appetite. The Duke of Anholt notwithstanding could not with-holde to aske Faustus with what reason there were such young fruite to be had at that time of yeare? Doctor Faustus tolde him, may it please your Grace to understand, that the yere is devided into two circles, that when with us it is Winter, in the contrary circle it is notwithstanding Sommer, for in India and Saba there falleth or setteth the Sunne, so that it is so warme, that they have twise a year fruit: and gracious Lorde, I have a swift Spirit, the which can in the twinckling of an eye fulfill my desire in any thing, wherefore I sent him into those Countries, who hath brought this fruite as you see: whereat the Duke was in great admiration.

Chapter 45

The Sunday following came these students home to Doctor Faustus his owne house, and brought their meate and drinke with them; these men were right welcome guests unto Faustus, wherfore they all fell to drinking of the wine smoothly: and being merry, they began some of them to talke of the beauty of women, and every one gave forth his verdit of what he had seene and what he had heard. So one among the rest said, I never was so desirous of any thing in this world, as to have a sight (if it were possible) of fayre Helena of Greece, for whome the worthy towne of Troie was destroyed and razed downe to the ground, therefore sayth hee, that in all mens judgement she was more than common fayre, because that when she was stolne away from her husband, there was for her recovery so great blood-shed.

Doctor Faustus answered: For that you are all my friends and are so desirous to see that famous pearle of Greece, fayre Helena ... I will therefor bring her into your presence personally, and in the same forme of attyre as she used to goe when she was in her chiefest flower and pleasauntest prime of youth ... but (sayd Doctor Faustus) I charge you all that upon your perils you speake not a word, nor rise up from the Table as long as she is in your presence. And so he went out of the Hall, returning presently agayne, after whome immediatly followed the fayre and beautiful Helena, whose beauty was such that the students were all amazed to see her, esteeming her rather to bee a heavenly than an earthly creature ...

Chapter 48

A good Christian an honest and vertuous olde man, a lover of the holy scriptures, who was neighbour unto Dr Faustus: when he perceived that many students had their recourse in and out unto Doctor Faustus, he suspected his evill life ... and ... began with these words. My loving friend and neighbour Doctor Faustus ... oh consider what you have done, it is not onely the pleasure of the body, but the safety of the soule that you must have respect unto ... But yet is it time enough Doctor Faustus, if you repent and call unto the Lord for mercy ... let my rude Sermon be unto you a conversion; and forget the filthy life that you have led, repent, aske mercy, and live ... Doctor Faustus heard him very attentively, and replyed. Father, your perswasions like me wondrous well, and I thanke you with all my heart for your good will and counsell ... And ... he layd him very pensive on his bed, bethinking himselfe of the words of the good olde man, and in a maner began to repent that he had given his Soule to the Divell, intending to denie all that hee had promised unto Lucifer. Continuing in these cogitations, sodainely his Spirit appeared ... saying unto him, Thou knowest Faustus that thou hast given thy selfe body and soule unto my Lord Lucifer ... wherefore he hath sent me unto thee, to tell thee, that seeing thou hast sorrowed for that thou hast done, begin againe and write another writing with thine owne blood, if not, then will I teare thee all to peeces. Hereat Doctor Faustus was sore afrayde, and sayd: My Mephostophiles, I will write agayne what thou wilt ...

Chapter 49

... And presently ... he became so great an enemie unto the poore olde man, that he sought his life by all meanes possible; but this godly man was strong in the holy Ghost, that he could not be vanquished by any meanes ...

Chapter 55

... To the ende that this miserable Faustus might fill the lust of his flesh ... he had a great desire to lie with fayre Helena of Greece ... Whereupon he called unto him his Spirit Mephostophiles, commanding him to bring him the faire Helena, which he also did. Whereupon he fell in love with her, and made her his common Concubine and bedfellow ...

Chapter 56

Doctor Faustus was now in his 24 and last yeare, and hee had a pretty stripling to his servant, the which had studied also at the Universitie of Wittenberg: this youth was very well acquainted with his knaveries and sorceries, so that hee was hated as well for his owne knaveries, as also for his Masters ... And when the time drew nigh that Faustus should end, hee called unto him a Notary and certaine masters the which were his friends and often conversant with him, in whose presence he gave this Wagner his house and Garden ...

Chapter 61

[Faustus bewailed his fate.] Nowe thou Faustus, damned wretch, howe happy wert thou if as an unreasonable beast thou mightest die without soule, so shouldest thou not feel any more doubts . . .

Chapter 63

[Faustus confessed to the Students.] . . . to the end that I might the better bring my purpose to passe, to have the Divels ayd and furtherance, which I never have wanted in mine actions, I have promised unto him at the ende and accomplishing of 24 yeares, both body and soule, to doe therewith at his pleasure: and this day, this dismall day those 24 yeare are fully expired . . . out of doubt hee will fetch mee . . .

. . . the Students wondered greatly . . . wherefore one of them sayd unto him; ah friend Faustus, what have you done to conceale this matter so long from us, we would by the help of good Divines, and the grace of God, have brought you out of this net . . . Doctor Faustus answered, I durst never doo it, although I often minded, to settle my selfe unto godly people, to desire counsell and helpe, as once mine olde neighbour counsailed mee, that I shoulde follow his learning, and leave all my conjurations, yet when I was minded to amend, and to follow that good mans counsell, then came the Divell and would have had me away, as this night he is like to doe, and sayd so soone as I turned againe to God, hee would dispatch me altogether . . .

. . . The Students and other that were there, when they had prayed for him, they wept, and so went foorth, but Faustus taryed in the hall . . . the Students lay neere unto that hall wherein Doctor Faustus lay, and they heard a mighty noyse and hissing, as if the hall had beene full of Snakes and Adders: with that the hall doore flew open wherein Doctor Faustus was, then he began to crie for helpe, saying murther, murther, but it cam foorth with halfe a voyce hollowly: shortly after they heard him no more.

APPENDIX B: THE 'ADICYONES' IN THE B TEXT

In 1616 an edition of *Dr Faustus* was published which was substantially different from all the previous editions. Most of the comic scenes had been altered, perhaps to suit Jacobean tastes which were more sophisticated than the Elizabethan ones had been. A stricter censorship had to be observed, following the punitive Act of Abuses in 1606. And the play now had to accommodate the extra material which cost £4 in 1602 when Henslowe recorded the payment in his *Diary*: 'unto Wm Burde & Samwell Rowle for ther adicyones in doctor fostes'.

This Appendix (which includes a revised list of *Dramatis Personae*) contains the scenes which underwent the most drastic revision; they are identified by the numbers of the scenes in the main text which they expand or replace. The same principles of presentation (capitalization, use of italic, and modernization of i/j and u/v) obtain here as there.

Dramatis Personae

Since there are so many differences in the *dramatis personae* of the A and B texts, it seems sensible to offer a separate 'cast list' for the two texts. Once again, the practice of modern theatre programmes is followed, and the *personae* are listed 'in order of appearance'.

Chorus
Dr John Faustus
Wagner
Angel (Good Angel)
Spirit (Bad Angel)
Valdes
Cornelius
Two Scholars
Lucifer
Mephostophilis
Clown
Belzebub
Seven Deadly Sins
    Pride
    Covetousness
    Envy
    Wrath
    Gluttony
    Sloth
    Lechery
Robin
Dick
Pope Adrian
Raymond King of Hungary

Pope Bruno
Two Cardinals (of France and
    Padua)
Archbishop of Rheims
Friars
Vintner
Martino
Frederick
Two Soldiers
Benvolio
Charles, Emperor of Germany
Duke of Saxony
Horse-courser
Carter
Hostess
Duke of Vanholt
Duchess of Vanholt
Third Scholar
Old Man
Devils, Attendants, Friars, Soldiers,
    and Spirits presenting Alexander
    the Great, his Paramour, Darius,
    and Helen of Troy

The Tragicall History
of the Life and Death
of *Doctor Faustus.*

Written by *Ch.* *Marklin*.

LONDON,
Printed for *Iohn Wright*, and are to be sold at his shop
without Newgate, at the s⸺ of ⸺he
Bi⸺ 1616.

[Scene 4]

Enter WAGNER *and the* CLOWNE.

WAGNER. Come hither sirra boy.

CLOWN. Boy? O disgrace to my person: Zounds boy in your face,
you have seen many boyes with beards I am sure.

WAGNER. Sirra, hast thou no commings In?

CLOWN. Yes, and goings out too, you may see sir.   5

WAGNER. Alas poore slave, see how poverty jests in his naked-
nesse, I know the Villaines out of service, and so hungry, that I
know he would give his soule to the devill, for a shoulder of
Mutton, tho it were bloud raw.

CLOWN. Not so neither; I had need to have it well rosted, and good   10
sauce to it, if I pay so deere, I can tell you.

WAGNER. Sirra, wilt thou be my man and waite on me? and I will
make thee go, like *Qui mihi discipulus.*

CLOWN. What, in Verse?

WAGNER. No slave, in beaten silke, and staves-aker.   15

CLOWN. Staves-aker? that's good to kill Vermine: then belike if I
serve you, I shall be lousy.

WAGNER. Why so thou shalt be, whether thou dost it or no: for
sirra, if thou dost not presently bind thy selfe to me for seven
yeares, I'le turne all the lice about thee into Familiars, and make   20
them tare thee in peeces.

CLOWN. Nay sir, you may save your selfe a labour, for they are as
familiar with me, as if they payd for their meate and drinke, I can
tell you.

WAGNER. Well sirra, leave your jesting, and take these Guilders.   25

CLOWN. Yes marry sir, and I thanke you to.

WAGNER. So, now thou art to bee at an howres warning, whensoever, and wheresoever the devill shall fetch thee.

CLOWN. Here, take your Guilders I'le none of 'em.

WAGNER. Not I, thou art Prest, prepare thy selfe, for I will pres-   30
ently raise up two devils to carry thee away: *Banio, Belcher.*

CLOWN. *Belcher?* and *Belcher* come here, I'le belch him: I am not
afraid of a devill.

Enter 2 devils.

WAGNER. How now sir will you serve me now?

CLOWN. I good *Wagner* take away the devill then.   35

WAGNER. Spirits away; now sirra follow me.

CLOWN. I will sir; but hearke you Maister, will you teach me this
conjuring Occupation?

WAGNER. I sirra, I'le teach thee to turne thy selfe to a Dog, or a
    Cat, or a Mouse, or a Rat, or any thing.   40
CLOWN. A Dog, or a Cat, or a Mouse, or a Rat? O brave *Wagner*.
WAGNER. Villaine, call me Maister *Wagner*, and see that you walke
    attentively, and let your right eye be alwaies, Diametrally fixt
    upon my left heele, that thou maist, *Quasi vestigias nostras insistere.*
CLOWN. Well sir, I warrant you.   45

                                                         Exeunt.

[Scene 6]

Enter the CLOWNE [ROBIN].

ROBIN. What *Dick*, looke to the horses there till I come againe. I
    have gotten one of Doctor *Faustus* conjuring bookes, and now
    we'le have such knavery, as't passes.

Enter DICK.

DICK. What *Robin*, you must come away & walk the horses.
ROBIN. I walke the horses, I scorn't 'faith, I have other matters in   5
    hand, let the horses walk themselves and they will. A *perse* a, t. h. e
    the: o *per se* o *deny orgon, gorgon*: keepe further from me O thou
    illiterate, and unlearned Hostler.
DICK. 'Snayles, what hast thou got there a book? why thou canst not
    tell ne're a word on't.   10
ROBIN. That thou shalt see presently: keep out of the circle, I say,
    least I send you into the Ostry with a vengeance.
DICK. That's like 'faith: you had best leave your foolery, for an my
    Maister come, he'le conjure you 'faith.
ROBIN. My Maister conjure me? I'le tell thee what, an my Maister   15
    come here, I'le clap as faire a paire of hornes on's head as e're thou
    sawest in thy life.
DICK. Thou needst not do that, for my Mistresse hath done it.
ROBIN. I, there be of us here, that have waded as deepe into
    matters, as other men, if they were disposed to talke.   20
DICK. A plague take you, I thought you did not sneake up and
    downe after her for nothing. But I prethee tell me, in good sad-
    nesse *Robin*, is that a conjuring booke?
ROBIN. Do but speake what thou't have me to do, and I'le do't: If
    thou't dance naked, put off thy cloathes, and I'le conjure thee   25
    about presently: Or if thou't go but to the Taverne with me, I'le
    give thee white wine, red wine, claret wine, Sacke, Muskadine,

Malmesey and Whippincrust, hold belly hold, and wee'le not pay
one peny for it.

DICK. O brave, prethee let's to it presently, for I am as dry as a dog.   30

ROBIN. Come then let's away.

Exeunt.

[Scene 7; lines added after 'Come therefore lets away' (line 49)]

MEPHOSTOPHILIS. Nay stay my *Faustus*: I know you'd see the Pope
And take some part of holy *Peters* feast,
The which this day with high solemnity,
This day is held through *Rome* and *Italy*,
In honour of the Popes triumphant victory.   5

FAUSTUS. Sweete *Mephostophilis* thou pleasest me:
Whilst I am here on earth let me be cloyd
With all things that delight the heart of man.
My foure and twenty yeares of liberty
I'le spend in pleasure and in daliance,   10
That *Faustus* name, whilst this bright frame doth stand,
May be admired through the furthest Land.

MEPHOSTOPHILIS. 'Tis well said *Faustus*, come then stand by me
And thou shalt see them come immediately.

FAUSTUS. Nay stay my gentle *Mephostophilis*,   15
And grant me my request, and then I go.
Thou know'st within the compasse of eight daies,
We view'd the face of heaven, of earth and hell.
So high our Dragons soar'd into the aire,
That looking downe the earth apppear'd to me,   20
No bigger then my hand in quantity.
There did we view the Kingdomes of the world,
And what might please mine eyes, I there beheld.
Then in this shew let me an Actor be,
That this proud Pope may *Faustus* cunning see.   25

MEPHOSTOPHILIS. Let it be so my *Faustus*, but first stay,
And view their triumphs, as they passe this way.
And then devise what best contents thy minde,
By cunning in thine Art to crosse the Pope,
Or dash the pride of this solemnity;   30
To make his Monkes and Abbots stand like Apes,
And point like Antiques at his triple Crowne:
To beate the beades about the Friers Pates,

Or clap huge hornes, upon the Cardinals heads:
Or any villany thou canst devise,   35
And I'le performe it *Faustus*: heark they come:
This day shall make thee be admir'd in *Rome*.

Enter the CARDINALS *and Bishops, some bearing Crosiers, some
the Pillars, Monkes and Friers, singing their Procession:
Then the* POPE *and* RAYMOND *King of* Hungary,
with BRUNO *led in chaines.*

POPE. Cast downe our Foot-stoole.
RAYMOND. *Saxon Bruno* stoope,
   Whilst on thy backe his hollinesse ascends   40
   Saint *Peters* Chaire and State Pontificall.
BRUNO. Proud *Lucifer*, that State belongs to me:
   But thus I fall to *Peter*, not to thee.
POPE. To me and *Peter*, shalt thou groveling lie,
   And crouch before the Papall dignity: 45
   Sound Trumpets then, for thus Saint *Peters* Heire,
   From *Bruno's* backe, ascends Saint *Peters* Chaire.

     A Flourish while he ascends.

Thus, as the Gods, creepe on with feete of wool,
Long ere with Iron hands they punish men,
So shall our sleeping vengeance now arise,   50
And smite with death thy hated enterprise.
Lords Cardinals of *France* and *Padua*,
Go forth-with to our holy Consistory,
And read amongst the Statutes Decretall,
What by the holy Councell held at *Trent*,   55
The sacred Sinod hath decreed for him,
That doth assume the Papall government,
Without election, and a true consent:
Away and bring us word with speed.
1 CARDINAL. We go my Lord.   *Exeunt* CARDINALS.
POPE. Lord *Raymond*.
FAUSTUS. Go hast thee gentle *Mephostophilis*,
   Follow the Cardinals to the Consistory;
   And as they turne their superstitious Bookes,
   Strike them with sloth, and drowsy idlenesse;   65
   And make them sleepe so sound, that in their shapes,
   Thy selfe and I, may parly with this Pope,
   This proud confronter of the Emperour:
   And in despite of all his Holinesse

Restore this *Bruno* to his liberty,   70
And beare him to the States of *Germany*.
MEPHOSTOPHILIS. *Faustus*, I goe.
FAUSTUS. Dispatch it soone,
The Pope shall curse that *Faustus* came to *Rome*.

Exit FAUSTUS *and* MEPH.

BRUNO. Pope *Adrian* let me have some right of Law,   75
I was elected by the Emperour.
POPE. We will depose the Emperour for that deed,
And curse the people that submit to him;
Both he and thou shalt stand excommunicate,
And interdict from Churches priviledge,   80
And all society of holy men:
He growes to prowd in his authority,
Lifting his loftie head above the clouds,
And like a Steeple over-peeres the Church.
But wee'le pul downe his haughty insolence: 85
And as Pope *Alexander* our Progenitour,
Trode on the neck of *Germane Fredericke*,
Adding this golden sentence to our praise;
That *Peters* heires should tread on Emperours,
And walke upon the dreadfull Adders backe,   90
Treading the Lyon, and the Dragon downe.
And fearelesse spurne the killing Basiliske:
So will we quell that haughty Schismatique;
And by authority Apostolicall
Depose him from his Regall Gouernment.   95
BRUNO. Pope *Julius* swore to Princely *Sigismond*,
For him, and the succeeding Popes of *Rome*,
To hold the Emperours their lawfull Lords.
POPE. Pope *Julius* did abuse the Churches Rites,
And therefore none of his Decrees can stand.   100
Is not all power on earth bestowed on us?
And therefore tho we would we cannot erre.
Behold this Silver Belt whereto is fixt
Seven golden seales fast sealed with seven seales,
In token of our seven-fold power from heaven,   105
To binde or loose, lock fast, condemne, or judge,
Resigne, or seale, or what so pleaseth us.
Then he and thou, and all the world shall stoope,
Or be assured of our dreadfull curse,
To light as heavy as the paines of hell.   110

Enter FAUSTUS *and* MEPHOSTO. *like the Cardinals.*

MEPHOSTOPHILIS. Now tell me *Faustus*, are we not fitted well?
FAUSTUS. Yes *Mephostophilis* and two such Cardinals
    Ne're serv'd a holy Pope, as we shall do.
    But whilst they sleepe within the Consistory,
    Let us salute his reverend Father-hood.   115
RAYMOND. Behold my Lord, the Cardinals are return'd.
POPE. Welcome grave Fathers, answere presently,
    What have our holy Councell there decreed,
    Concerning *Bruno* and the Emperour,
    In quittance of their late conspiracie   120
    Against our State, and Papall dignitie?
FAUSTUS. Most sacred Patron of the Church of *Rome*,
    By full consent of all the Synod
    Of Priests and Prelates, it is thus decreed:
    That *Bruno*, and the *Germane* Emperour   125
    Be held as Lollards, and bold Schismatiques,
    And proud disturbers of the Churches peace.
    And if that *Bruno* by his owne assent,
    Without inforcement of the *German* Peeres,
    Did seeke to weare the triple Dyadem,   130
    And by your death to clime S. *Peters* Chaire,
    The Statutes Decretall have thus decreed,
    He shall be streight condemn'd of heresie,
    And on a pile of Fagots burnt to death.
POPE. It is enough: there, take him to your charge,   135
    And beare him streight to *Ponto Angelo*,
    And in the strongest Tower inclose him fast,
    To morrow, sitting in our Consistory,
    With all our Colledge of grave Cardinals,
    We will determine of his life or death.   140
    Here, take his triple Crowne along with you,
    And leave it in the Churches treasury.
    Make haste againe, my good Lord Cardinalls,
    And take our blessing Apostolicall.
MEPHOSTOPHILIS. So, so, was never Divell thus blest before. 145
FAUSTUS. Away sweet *Mephostophilis*, be gone,
    The Cardinals will be plagu'd for this anon.
                        Ex. FA & MEP.

POPE. Go presently, and bring a banket forth,
    That we may solemnize S. *Peters* feast,
    And with Lord *Raymond*, King of *Hungary*,   150
    Drinke to our late and happy victory.   *Exeunt.*

A Senit while the Banquet is brought in; and then Enter
FAUSTUS *and* MEPHASTOPHILIS *in their owne shapes.*

MEPHOSTOPHILIS. Now *Faustus*, come prepare thy selfe for mirth,
    The sleepy Cardinals are hard at hand,
    To censure *Bruno*, that is posted hence,
    And on a proud pac'd Steed, as swift as thought,   155
    Flies ore the Alpes to fruitfull *Germany*,
    There to salute the wofull Emperour.
FAUSTUS. The Pope will curse them for their sloth to day.
    That slept both *Bruno* and his crowne away,
    But now, that *Faustus* may delight his minde,   160
    And by their folly make some merriment,
    Sweet *Mephastophilis* so charme me here,
    That I may walke invisible to all,
    And doe what ere I please, unseene of any.
MEPHOSTOPHILIS. *Faustus* thou shalt, then kneele downe presently,165
    Whilst on thy head I lay my hand,
    And charme thee with this Magicke wand,
    First weare this girdle, then appeare
    Invisible to all are here:
    The Planets seven, the gloomy aire,   170
    Hell and the Furies forked haire,
    Pluto's blew fire, and Hecat's tree,
    With Magicke spels so compasse thee,
    That no eye may thy body see.
    So *Faustus*, now for all their holinesse,   175
    Do what thou wilt, thou shalt not be discern'd.
FAUSTUS. Thankes *Mephastophilis*: now Friers take heed,
    Lest *Faustus* make your shaven crownes to bleed.
MEPHOSTOPHILIS. *Faustus* no more: see where the Cardinals come.

Enter POPE *and all the Lords. Enter the* CARDINALS
with a Booke.

POPE. Welcome Lord Cardinals: come sit downe.   180
    Lord *Raymond*, take your seate, Friers attend,
    And see that all things be in readinesse,
    As best beseemes this solemne festivall.
1 CARDINAL. First, may it please your sacred Holinesse,
    To view the sentence of the reverend Synod,   185
    Concerning *Bruno* and the Emperour.
POPE. What needs this question? Did I not tell you,
    To morrow we would sit i'th Consistory,

And there determine of his punishment?
You brought us word even now, it was decreed,   190
That *Bruno* and the cursed Emperour
Were by the holy Councell both condemn'd
For lothed Lollords, and base Schismatiques:
Then wherefore would you have me view that booke?

1 CARDINAL. Your Grace mistakes, you gave us no such charge.   195

RAYMOND. Deny it not, we all are witnesses
    That *Bruno* here was late delivered you,
    With his rich triple crowne to be reserv'd,
    And put into the Churches treasury.

AMBO CARDINALS. By holy *Paul* we saw them not.   200

POPE. By *Peter* you shall dye,
    Unlesse you bring them forth immediatly:
    Hale them to prison, lade their limbes with gyves:
    False Prelates, for this hatefull treachery,
    Curst be your soules to hellish misery.   205

FAUSTUS. So, they are safe: now *Faustus* to the feast,
    The Pope had never such a frolicke guest.

POPE. Lord Archbishop of *Reames*, sit downe with us.

BISHOP. I thanke your Holinesse.

FAUSTUS. Fall to, the Divell choke you an you spare.   210

POPE. Who's that spoke? Friers looke about,
    Lord *Raymond* pray fall too, I am beholding
    To the Bishop of *Millaine*, for this so rare a present.

FAUSTUS. I thanke you sir.

POPE. How now? who snatch't the meat from me?   215
    Villaines why speake you not?
    My good Lord Archbishop, heres a most daintie dish,
    Was sent me from a Cardinall in *France*.

FAUSTUS. I'le have that too.

POPE. What Lollards do attend our Hollinesse,   220
    That we receive such great indignity? fetch me some wine.

FAUSTUS. I, pray do, for *Faustus* is a dry.

POPE. Lord *Raymond*, I drink unto your grace.

FAUSTUS. I pledge your grace.

POPE. My wine gone too? yee Lubbers look about   225
    And find the man that doth this villany,
    Or by our sanctitude you all shall die.
    I pray my Lords have patience at this
    Troublesome banquet.

BISHOP. Please it your holinesse, I thinke it be some Ghost crept   230
    out of Purgatory, and now is come unto your holinesse for his
    pardon.

POPE. It may be so:
　　Go then command our Priests to sing a Dirge,
　　To lay the fury of this same troublesome ghost.
FAUSTUS. How now? must every bit be spiced with a Crosse?　　235
　　Nay then take that.
POPE. O I am slaine, help me my Lords:
　　O come and help to beare my body hence:
　　Damb'd be this soule for ever, for this deed.
　　　　　　　　　　　　　　　　Exeunt the POPE *and his traine.*
MEPHOSTOPHILIS. Now *Faustus*, what will you do now? for I can tell you
　　You'le be curst with Bell, Booke and Candle.
FAUSTUS. Bell, Booke, and Candle; Candle, Booke, and Bell,
　　Forward and backward, to curse *Faustus* to hell.

　　　　Enter the FRIERS *with Bell, Booke, and Candle,*
　　　　　　　　　　for the Dirge.

I FRIAR. Come brethren, let's about our business with good devotion.

　　Cursed be he that stole his holinesse meate from the Table.　　245

　　　　　　　　Maledicat Dominus.

　　Cursed be he that stroke his holinesse a blow on the face.

　　　　　　　　Maledicat Dominus.

　　Cursed be he that strucke fryer *Sandelo* a blow on the pate.

　　　　　　　　Maledicat Dom.　　　　　250

　　Cursed be he that disturbeth our holy Dirge.

　　　　　　　　Maledicat Dom.

　　Cursed be that he tooke away his holinesse wine.

　　　　　　　　Maledicat Dom.

　　　　Beate the FRIERS, *fling fire worke among them,*
　　　　　　　　and Exeunt.

[Scene 8]

Enter CLOWNE [ROBIN] *and* DICKE, *with a Cup.*

DICK. Sirra *Robin*, we were best looke that your devill can answere
　　the stealing of this same cup, for the Vintners boy followes us at
　　the hard heeles.

ROBIN. 'Tis no matter, let him come; an he follow us, I'le so conjure him, as he was never conjur'd in his life, I warrant him: let me   5
see the cup.

Enter VINTNER.

DICK. Here 'tis: Yonder he comes: Now *Robin*, now or never shew
thy cunning.

VINTNER. O, are you here? I am glad I have found you, you are a
couple of fine companions: pray where's the cup you stole from   10
the Taverne?

ROBIN. How, how? we steale a cup? take heed what you say, we
looke not like cup-stealers I can tell you.

VINTNER. Never deny't, for I know you have it, and I'le search
you.   15

ROBIN. Search me? I and spare not: hold the cup *Dick*, come, come,
search me, search me.

VINTNER. Come on sirra, let me search you now.

DICK. I, I, do, do, hold the cup *Robin*, I feare not your searching;
we scorne to steale your cups I can tell you.   20

VINTNER. Never out face me for the matter, for sure the cup is
betweene you two.

ROBIN. Nay there you lie, 'tis beyond us both.

VINTNER. A plague take you, I thought 'twas your knavery to take
it away: Come, give it me againe.   25

ROBIN. I much, when can you tell: *Dick* make me a circle and stand
close at my backe, and stir not for thy life, *Vintner* you shall have
your cup anon, say nothing *Dick*: *O per se o, demogorgon Belcher*
and *Mephostophilis*

Enter MEPHOSTOPHILIS.

MEPHOSTOPHILIS. You Princely Legions of infernall Rule,   30
How am I vexed by these villaines Charmes?
From *Constantinople* have they brought me now,
Onely for pleasure of these damned slaves.

ROBIN. By Lady sir, you have had a shroud journey of it, will it
please you to take a shoulder of Mutton to supper, and a Tester in   35
your purse, and go back againe.

DICK. I, I pray you heartily sir; for wee cal'd you but in jest I
promise you.

MEPHOSTOPHILIS. To purge the rashnesse of this cursed deed,
First, be thou turned to this ugly shape,   40
For Apish deeds transformed to an Ape.

ROBIN. O brave, an Ape? I pray sir, let me have the carrying of him
about to shew some trickes.

MEPHOSTOPHILIS. And so thou shalt: be thou transform'd to a
  dog, and carry him upon thy backe; away be gone.   45
ROBIN. A dog? that's excellent: let the Maids looke well to their
  porridge-pots, for I'le into the Kitchin presently: come *Dick*,
  come.

                                        Exeunt the two Clownes.

MEPHOSTOPHILIS. Now with the flames of ever-burning fire,
  I'le wing my selfe and forth-with flie amaine   50
  Unto my *Faustus* to the great Turkes Court.

                                                    Exit.

[Scene 9]

Enter MARTINO *and* FREDERICKE *at severall dores.*

MARTINO. What ho, Officers, Gentlemen,
  Hye to the presence to attend the Emperour,
  Good *Fredericke* see the roomes be voyded straight,
  His Majesty is comming to the Hall;
  Go backe, and see the State in readinesse.   5
FREDERICK. But where is *Bruno* our elected Pope,
  That on a furies back came post from *Rome*,
  Will not his grace consort the Emperour.
MARTINO. O yes, and with him comes the *Germane* Conjurer.
  The learned *Faustus*, fame of *Wittenberge*,   10
  The wonder of the world for Magick Art;
  And he intends to shew great *Carolus*,
  The race of all his stout progenitors;
  And bring in presence of his Majesty,
  The royall shapes and warlike semblances   15
  Of *Alexander* and his beauteous Paramour.
FREDERICK. Where is *Benvolio*?
MARTINO. Fast a sleepe I warrant you,
  He took his rouse with stopes of *Rhennish* wine,
  So kindly yesternight to *Bruno's* health,   20
  That all this day the sluggard keepes his bed.
FREDERICK. See, see his window's ope, we'l call to him.
MARTINO. What hoe, *Benvolio*.

              Enter BENVOLIO *above at a window,
                in his nightcap: buttoning.*

BENVOLIO. What a devill ayle you two?
MARTINO. Speak softly sir, least the devil heare you: 25

For *Faustus* at the Court is late arriv'd,
And at his heeles a thousand furies waite,
To accomplish what soever the Doctor please.
BENVOLIO. What of this?
MARTINO. Come leave thy chamber first, and thou shalt see   30
This Conjurer performe such rare exploits,
Before the Pope and royall Emperour,
As never yet was seene in *Germany*.
BENVOLIO. Has not the Pope enough of conjuring yet?
He was upon the devils backe late enough;   35
And if he be so farre in love with him,
I would he would post with him to *Rome* againe.
FREDERICK. Speake, wilt thou come and see this sport?
BENVOLIO. Not I.
MARTINO. Wilt thou stand in thy Window, and see it then?   40
BENVOLIO. I, and I fall not asleepe i'th' meane time.
MARTINO. The Emperour is at hand, who comes to see
What wonders by blacke spels may compast be.
BENVOLIO. Well, go you attend the Emperour: I am content for
this once to thrust my head out at a window: for they say, if a man   45
be drunke over night, the Divell cannot hurt him in the morning:
if that bee true, I have a charme in my head, shall controule him as
well as the Conjurer, I warrant you.

                                                 Exit.

A Senit. CHARLES *the Germane* EMPEROUR, BRUNO,
SAXONY, FAUSTUS, MEPHOSTOPHILIS,
FREDERICKE, MARTINO *and Attendants.*

EMPEROR. Wonder of men, renown'd Magitian,
Thrice learned *Faustus*, welcome to our Court.   50
This deed of thine, in setting *Bruno* free
From his and our professed enemy,
Shall adde more excellence unto thine Art,
Then if by powerfull Necromantick spels,
Thou couldst command the worlds obedience: 55
For ever be belov'd of *Carolus*.
And if this *Bruno* thou hast late redeem'd,
In peace possesse the triple Diadem,
And sit in *Peters* Chaire, despite of chance,
Thou shalt be famous through all *Italy*,   60
And honour'd of the *Germane* Emperour.
FAUSTUS. These gracious words, most royall *Carolus*,
Shall make poore *Faustus* to his utmost power,

Both love and serve the *Germane* Emperour,
And lay his life at holy *Bruno's* feet.   65
For proofe whereof, if so your Grace be pleas'd,
The Doctor stands prepar'd, by power of Art,
To cast his Magicke charmes, that shall pierce through
The Ebon gates of ever-burning hell,
And hale the stubborne Furies from their caves,   70
To compasse whatsoere your grace commands.

BENVOLIO. Bloud he speaks terribly: but for all that, I doe not
greatly beleeve him, he lookes as like Conjurer as the Pope to a
Coster-monger.

EMPEROR. Then *Faustus* as thou late didst promise us,   75
We would behold that famous Conqueror,
Great *Alexander*, and his Paramour,
In their true shapes, and state Majesticall,
That we may wonder at their excellence.

FAUSTUS. Your Majesty shall see them presently,   80
Mephostophilis away.
And with a solemne noyse of trumpets sound,
Present before this royall Emperour,
Great *Alexander* and his beauteous Paramour.

MEPHOSTOPHILIS. *Faustus* I will.   85
                                        [*exit* MEPHOSTOPHILIS.]

BENVOLIO. Well Master Doctor, an your Divels come not away
quickly, you shall have me asleepe presently: zounds I could eate
my selfe for anger, to thinke I have beene such an Asse all this
while, to stand gaping after the divels Governor, and can see
nothing.   90

FAUSTUS. Il'e make you feele something anon, if my Art faile me
not.
My Lord, I must forewarne your Majesty,
That when my Spirits present the royall shapes
Of *Alexander* and his Paramour,   95
Your grace demand no questions of the King,
But in dumbe silence let them come and goe.

EMPEROR. Be it as *Faustus* please, we are content.

BENVOLIO. I, I, and I am content too: and thou bring *Alexander*
and his Paramour before the Emperour, Il'e be *Acteon,* and turne   100
my selfe to a Stagge.

FAUSTUS. And Ile play *Diana*, and send you the hornes presently.
            Senit. Enter at one the Emperour Alexander, at the other
                Darius; they meete, Darius is throwne downe, Alexander
                    kils him; takes off his Crowne, and offering to goe

out, his Paramour meetes him, he embraceth her, and
sets Darius Crowne upon her head; and coming backe,
both salute the EMPEROUR *who leaving his State,*
offers to embrace them, which FAUSTUS *seeing,*
suddenly staies him.
Then trumpets cease, and Musicke sounds.

My gracious Lord, you doe forget your selfe,
These are but shadowes, not substantiall.

EMPEROR. O pardon me, my thoughts are so ravished   105
With sight of this renowned Emperour,
That in mine armes I would have compast him.
But *Faustus*, since I may not speake to them,
To satisfie my longing thoughts at full,
Let me this tell thee: I have heard it said,   110
That this faire Lady, whilest she liv'd on earth,
Had on her necke a little wart, or mole;
How may I prove that saying to be true?

FAUSTUS. Your Majesty may boldly goe and see.

EMPEROR. *Faustus* I see it plaine,   115
And in this sight thou better pleasest me,
Then if I gain'd another Monarchie.

FAUSTUS. Away, be gone   *Exit Show.*
See, see, my gracious Lord, what strange beast is yon,
That thrusts his head out at window.   120

EMPEROR. O wondrous sight: see Duke of *Saxony*,
Two spreading hornes most strangely fastened
Upon the head of yong *Benvolio*.

SAXONY. What is he asleepe, or dead?

FAUSTUS. He sleeps my Lord, but dreames not of his hornes.   125

EMPEROR. This sport is excellent: wee'l call and wake him. What
ho, *Benvolio*.

BENVOLIO. A plague upon you, let me sleepe a while.

EMPEROR. I blame thee not to sleepe much, having such a head of
thine owne.   130

SAXONY. Looke up *Benvolio*, tis the Emperour calls.

BENVOLIO. The Emperour? where? O zounds my head.

EMPEROR. Nay, and thy hornes hold, tis no matter for thy head, for
that's arm'd sufficiently.

FAUSTUS. Why how now sir Knight, what hang'd by the hornes?   135
this most horrible: fie, fie, pull in your head for shame, let not all
the world wonder at you.

BENVOLIO. Zounds Doctor, is this your villany?

FAUSTUS. O say not so sir: the Doctor has no skill,

No Art, no cunning, to present these Lords,   140
Or bring before this royall Emperour
The mightie Monarch, warlicke *Alexander*.
If *Faustus* do it, you are streight resolv'd,
In bold *Acteons* shape to turne a Stagge.
And therefore my Lord, so please your Majesty,   145
Il'e raise a kennell of Hounds shall hunt him so,
As all his footmanship shall scarce prevaile,
To keepe his Carkasse from their bloudy phangs.
Ho, *Belimote, Argiron, Asterote.*
BENVOLIO. Hold, hold: zounds hee'l raise up a kennell of Divels   150
I thinke anon: good my Lord intreate for me: 'sbloud I am never
able to endure these torments.
EMPEROR. Then good Master Doctor,
Let me intreate you to remove his hornes,
He has done penance now sufficiently.   155
FAUSTUS. My gracious Lord, not so much for injury done to me, as
to delight your Majesty with some mirth: hath *Faustus* justly
requited this injurious knight, which being all I desire, I am con-
tent to remove his hornes. *Mephastophilis*, transforme him; and
hereafter sir, looke you speake well of Schollers.   160
BENVOLIO. Speake well of yee? 'sbloud and Schollers be such
Cuckold-makers to clap hornes of honest mens heades o'this
order, Il'e nere trust smooth faces and small ruffes more. But an I
be not reveng'd for this, would I might be turn'd to a gaping
Oyster, and drinke nothing but salt water.   [*Exit.*]
EMPEROR. Come *Faustus* while the Emperour lives,
In recompence of this thy high desert,
Thou shalt command the state of *Germany*,
And live belov'd of mightie *Carolus*.

Exeunt omnes.

Enter BENVOLIO, MARTINO, FREDERICKE,
and Souldiers.

MARTINO. Nay sweet *Benvolio*, let us sway thy thoughts   170
From this attempt against the Conjurer.
BENVOLIO. Away, you love me not, to urge me thus,
Shall I let slip so great an injury,
When every servile groome jeasts at my wrongs,
And in their rusticke gambals proudly say,   175
Benvolio's head was grac't with hornes to day?
O may these eye-lids never close againe,
Till with my sword I have that Conjurer slaine.

If you will aid me in this enterprise,
Then draw your weapons, and be resolute: 180
If not, depart: here will *Benvolio* die,
But *Faustus* death shall quit my infamie.
FREDERICK. Nay, we will stay with thee, betide what may,
   And kill that Doctor if he come this way.
BENVOLIO. Then gentle *Fredericke* hie thee to the grove,   185
   And place our servants, and our followers
   Close in an ambush there behinde the trees,
   By this (I know) the Conjurer is neere,
   I saw him kneele, and kisse the Emperours hand,
   And take his leave, laden with rich rewards.   190
   Then Souldiers boldly fight; if *Faustus* die,
   Take you the wealth, leave us the victorie.
FREDERICK. Come souldiers, follow me unto the grove,
   Who kils him shall have gold, and endlesse love.
               Exit FREDERICKE *with the Souldiers.*
BENVOLIO. My head is lighter then it was by th'hornes,   195
   But yet my heart more ponderous then my head,
   And pants untill I see that Conjurer dead.
MARTINO. Where shall we place our selves *Benvolio*?
BENVOLIO. Here will we stay to bide the first assault,
   O were that damned Hell-hound but in place,   200
   Thou soone shouldst see me quit my foule disgrace.

               Enter FREDERICKE.

FREDERICK. Close, close, the Conjurer is at hand,
   And all alone, comes walking in his gowne;
   Be ready then, and strike the Peasant downe.
BENVOLIO. Mine be that honour then: now sword strike home,   205
   For hornes he gave, Il'e have his head anone.

               Enter FAUSTUS *with the false head.*

MARTINO. See, see, he comes.
BENVOLIO. No words: this blow ends all,
   Hell take his soule, his body thus must fall.
FAUSTUS. Oh.   210
FREDERICK. Grone you Master Doctor?
BENVOLIO. Breake may his heart with grones: deere *Frederik* see
   Thus will I end his griefes immediatly.
MARTINO. Strike with a willing hand, his head is off.
BENVOLIO. The Divel's dead, the Furies now may laugh   215
FREDERICK. Was this that sterne aspect, that awfull frowne,

Made the grim monarch of infernall spirits,
Tremble and quake at his commanding charmes?

MARTINO. Was this that damned head, whose heart conspir'd
Benvolio's shame before the Emperour.   220

BENVOLIO. I, that's the head, and here the body lies,
Justly rewarded for his villanies.

FREDERICK. Come, let's devise how we may adde more shame
To the blacke scandall of his hated name.

BENVOLIO. First, on his head, in quittance of my wrongs,   225
Il'e naile huge forked hornes, and let them hang
Within the window where he yoak'd me first,
That all the world may see my just revenge.

MARTINO. What use shall we put his beard to?

BENVOLIO. Wee'l sell it to a Chimny-sweeper: it will weare out ten   230
birchin broomes I warrant you.

FREDERICK. What shall eyes doe?

BENVOLIO. Wee'l put out his eyes, and they shall serve for buttons
to his lips, to keepe his tongue from catching cold.

MARTINO. An excellent policie: and now sirs, having divided him,   235
what shall the body doe?

> [FAUSTUS *stands up.*]

BENVOLIO. Zounds the Divel's alive agen.

FREDERICK. Give him his head for Gods sake.

FAUSTUS. Nay keepe it: *Faustus* will have heads and hands
I call your hearts to recompence this deed.   240
Knew you not Traytors, I was limitted
For foure and twenty yeares, to breathe on earth?
And had you cut my body with your swords,
Or hew'd this flesh and bones as small as sand,
Yet in a minute had my spirit return'd,   245
And I had breath'd a man made free from harme.
But wherefore doe I dally my revenge?
Asteroth, Belimoth, Mephostophilis,

> *Ent. Meph. & other Divels.*

Go horse these traytors on your fiery backes,
And mount aloft with them as high as heaven,   250
Thence pitch them headlong to the lowest hell:
Yet stay, the world shall see their miserie,
And hell shall after plague their treacherie.
Go *Belimothe*, and take this caitife hence,
And hurle him in some lake of mud and durt: 255

Take thou this other, dragge him through the woods,
Amongst the pricking thornes, and sharpest briers,
Whilst with my gentle *Mephostophilis,*
This Traytor flies unto some steepie rocke,
That rowling downe, may breake the villaines bones,   260
As he intended to dismember me.
Fly hence, dispatch my charge immediatly.
FREDERICK. Pitie us gentle *Faustus,* save our lives.
FAUSTUS. Away.
FREDERICK. He must needs goe that the Divell drives.   265
                    Exeunt Spirits with the KNIGHTS.

             Enter the ambusht SOULDIERS.

1 SOLDIER. Come sirs, prepare your selves in readinesse,
     Make hast to help these noble Gentlemen,
     I heard them parly with the Conjurer.
2 SOLDIER. See where he comes, dispatch, and kill the slave.
FAUSTUS. What's here? an ambush to betray my life: 270
     Then *Faustus* try thy skill: base pesants stand,
     For loe these Trees remove at my command,
     And stand as Bulwarkes twixt your selves and me,
     To sheild me from your hated treachery:
     Yet to encounter this your weake attempt,   275
     Beholde an Army comes incontinent.
     FAUSTUS *strikes the dore, and enter a devill playing on a Drum,*
          after him another bearing an Ensigne: and divers with
          weapons, MEPHOSTOPHILIS *with fire-workes; they set upon*
               the SOULDIERS *and drive them out.*

Enter at severall dores, BENVOLIO, FREDERICKE, *and* MARTINO,
          their heads and faces bloudy, and besmear'd with
               mud and durt; all having hornes on their heads.

MARTINO. What ho, *Benvolio.*
BENVOLIO. Here, what *Frederick,* ho.
FREDERICK. O help me gentle friend; where is *Martino?*
MARTINO. Deere *Frederick* here,   280
     Halfe smother'd in a Lake of mud and durt,
     Through which the Furies drag'd me by the heeles.
FREDERICK. *Martino* see,
     Benvolio's hornes againe.
MARTINO. O misery, how now *Benvolio?*   285
BENVOLIO. Defend me heaven, shall I be haunted still?
MARTINO. Nay feare not man we have no power to kill.

BENVOLIO. My friends transformed thus: O hellish spite,
    Your heads are all set with hornes.
FREDERICK. You hit it right,   290
    It is your owne you meane feele on your head.
BENVOLIO. 'Zons, hornes againe.
MARTINO. Nay chafe not man, we all are sped.
BENVOLIO. What devill attends this damn'd Magician,
    That spite of spite, our wrongs are doubled?   295
FREDERICK. What may we do, that we may hide our shames?
BENVOLIO. If we should follow him to worke revenge,
    He'd joyne long Asses eares to these huge hornes,
    And make us laughing stockes to all the world.
MARTINO. What shall we [do] then deere *Benvolio*?   300
BENVOLIO. I have a Castle joyning neere these woods,
    And thither wee'le repaire and live obscure,
    Till time shall alter this our brutish shapes.
    Sith blacke disgrace hath thus eclipst our fame:
    We'le rather die with griefe, then live with shame.   305

                             Exeunt omnes.

[Scene 10]

Enter FAUSTUS *and the* HORSE-COURSER,
and MEPHOSTOPHILIS.

HORSE-COURSER. I beseech your Worship accept of these forty
Dollors.
FAUSTUS. Friend, thou canst not buy so good a horse, for so small a
price: I have no great need to sell him, but if thou likest him for
ten Dollors more, take him, because I see thou hast a good minde   5
to him.
HORSE-COURSER. I beseech you sir accept of this; I am a very
poore man, and have lost very much of late by horse flesh, and this
bargaine will set me up againe.
FAUSTUS. Well, I will not stand with thee, give me the money: now   10
sirra I must tell you, that you may ride him o'er hedge and ditch,
and spare him not; but do you heare? in any case, ride him not into
the water.
HORSE-COURSER. How, sir, not into the water? why will he not
drink of all waters?   15
FAUSTUS. Yes, he will drinke of all waters, but ride him not into
the water: o're hedge and ditch, or where thou wilt, but not into

the water: Go bid the Hostler deliver him unto you, and remember what I say.

HORSE-COURSER. I warrant you sir; O joyfull day: Now am I a   20
made man for ever.   *Exit.*

FAUSTUS. What art thou *Faustus* but a man condemn'd to die?
Thy fatall time drawes to a finall end;
Despaire doth drive distrust into my thoughts.
Confound these passions with a quiet sleepe: 25
Tush *Christ* did call the Theefe upon the Crosse,
Then rest thee *Faustus* quiet in conceit.
                                          He sits to sleepe.

Enter the HORSE-COURSER *wet.*

HORSE-COURSER. O what a cosening Doctor was this? I riding
my horse into the water, thinking some hidden mystery had beene
in the horse, I had nothing under me but a little straw, and had   30
much ado to escape drowning: Well I'le go rouse him, and make
him give me my forty Dollors againe. Ho sirra Doctor, you coson-
ing scab; Maister Doctor awake, and rise, and give me my mony
againe, for your horse is turned to a bottle of Hay,——Maister
Doctor.   35
                                        He puls off his leg.

Alas I am undone, what shall I do? I have puld off his leg.

FAUSTUS. O help, help, the villaine hath murder'd me.

HORSE-COURSER. Murder or not murder, now he has but one leg,
I'le out-run him, and cast this leg into some ditch or other.

FAUSTUS. Stop him, stop him, stop him——ha, ha, ha, *Faustus*   40
hath his leg againe, and the Horse-courser a bundle of hay for his
forty Dollors.

Enter WAGNER.

How now *Wagner* what newes with thee?

WAGNER. If it please you, the Duke of *Vanholt* doth earnestly
entreate your company, and hath sent some of his men to attend   45
you with provision fit for your journey.

FAUSTUS. The Duke of *Vanholt's* an honourable Gentleman, and
one to whom I must be no niggard of my cunning; Come away.
                                          Exeunt.

[Scene 11]

Enter CLOWNE [ROBIN], DICK, HORSE-COURSER *and a*
CARTER.

CARTER. Come my Maisters, I'le bring you to the best beere in
Europe, what ho, Hostis; where be these Whores?

Enter HOSTIS.

HOSTESS. How now, what lacke you? What my old Guesse welcome.

CLOWN. Sirra *Dick*, dost thou know why I stand so mute?

DICK. No *Robin*, why is't?   5

CLOWN. I am eighteene pence on the score, but say nothing, see if
she have forgotten me.

HOSTESS. Who's this, that stands so solemnly by himselfe: what my
old Guest?

CLOWNE. O Hostisse how do you? I hope my score stands still.   10

HOSTESS. I there's no doubt of that, for me thinkes you make no
hast to wipe it out.

DICK. Why Hostesse, I say, fetch us some Beere.

HOSTESS. You shall presently: looke up into th'hall there ho.

Exit.

DICK. Come sirs, what shall we do now till mine Hostesse comes?   15

CARTER. Marry sir, I'le tell you the bravest tale how a Conjurer
serv'd me; you know Doctor *Fauster*.

HORSE-COURSER. I, a plague take him, heere's some on's have
cause to know him; did he conjure thee too?

CARTER. I'le tell you how he serv'd me: As I was going to *Witten-*   20
berge t'other day, with a loade of Hay, he met me, and asked me
what he should give me for as much Hay as he could eate; now sir,
I thinking that a little would serve his turne, bad him take as much
as he would for three-farthings; so he presently gave me my mony,
and fell to eating; and as I am a cursen man, he never left eating,   25
till he had eate up all my loade of Hay.

ALL. O monstrous, eate a whole load of Hay!

CLOWN. Yes, Yes, that may be; for I have heard of one, that ha's
eate a load of logges.

HORSE-COURSER. Now sirs, you shall heare how villanously he   30
serv'd mee: I went to him yesterday to buy a horse of him, and he
would by no meanes sell him under 40 Dollors; so sir, because I
knew him to be such a horse, as would run over hedge and ditch,
and never tyre, I gave him his money; so when I had my horse,
Doctor *Fauster* bad me ride him night and day, and spare him no   35
time; but, quoth he, in any case ride him not into the water. Now

sir, I thinking the horse had had some quality that he would not
have me know of, what did I but rid him into a great river, and
when I came just in the midst my horse vanisht away, and I sate
straddling upon a bottle of Hay.   40

ALL. O brave Doctor.

HORSE-COURSER. But you shall heare how bravely I serv'ed him
for it; I went me home to his house, and there I found him asleepe;
I kept a hallowing and whooping in his eares, but all could not
wake him: I seeing that, tooke him by the leg, and never rested   45
pulling, till I had pul'd me his leg quite off, and now 'tis at home
in mine Hostry.

CLOWN. And has the Doctor but one leg then? that's excellent, for
one of his devils turn'd me, into the likenesse of an Apes face.

CARTER. Some more drinke Hostesse.   50

CLOWN. Hearke you, we'le into another roome and drinke a while,
and then we'le go seeke out the Doctor.

Exeunt omnes.

Enter the DUKE *of Vanholt; his* DUTCHES,
FAUSTUS, *and* MEPHOSTOPHILIS [*and a* SERVANT].

DUKE. Thankes Maister Doctor, for these pleasant sights,
Nor know I how sufficiently to recompence your great deserts in
erecting that inchanted Castle in the Aire: 55
The sight whereof so delighted me
As nothing in the world could please me more.

FAUSTUS. I do thinke my selfe my good Lord, highly recom-
penced, in that it pleaseth your grace to thinke but well of that
which *Faustus* hath performed. But gratious Lady, it may be, that 60
you have taken no pleasure in those sights; therefor I pray you tell
me, what is the thing you most desire to have, be it in the world, it
shall be yours: I have heard that great bellyed women, do long for
things, are rare and dainty.

DUCHESS. True Maister Doctor, and since I finde you so kind I   65
will make knowne unto you what my heart desires to have, and
were it now Summer, as it is January, a dead time of the Winter, I
would request no better meate, then a dish of ripe grapes.

FAUSTUS. This is but a small matter: Go *Mephostophilis*, away.

Exit MEPHOSTO.

Madam, I will do more then this for your content.   70

Enter MEPH. *agen with the grapes.*

Here, now taste yee these, they should be good
For they come from a farre Country I can tell you.

DUKE. This makes me wonder more then all the rest, that at this
time of the yeare, when every Tree is barren of his fruite, from
whence you had these ripe grapes.   75
FAUSTUS. Please it your grace, the yeare is divided into two circles
over the whole world, so that when it is Winter with us, in the
contrary circle it is likewise Summer with them, as in *India*, *Saba*,
and such Countries that lye farre East, where they have fruit twice
a yeare. From whence, by meanes of a swift spirit that I have, I   80
had these grapes brought as you see.
DUCHESS. And trust me, they are the sweetest grapes that e're I
tasted.

> The CLOWNES [ROBIN, DICK, CARTER, HORSE-COURSER]
> *bounce at the gate, within.*

DUKE. What rude disturbers have we at the gate?
Go pacifie their fury set it ope,   85
And then demand of them, what they would have.

> *They knocke againe, and call out to talke with* FAUSTUS
> [*within.*]

SERVANT. Why how now Maisters, what a coyle is there?
What is the reason you disturbe the Duke?
DICK. We have no reason for it, therefore a fig for him.
SERVANT. Why saucy varlets, dare you be so bold.   90
HORSE-COURSER. I hope sir, we have wit enough to be more bold
then welcome.
SERVANT. It appeares so, pray be bold else-where,
And trouble not the Duke.
DUKE. What would they have?   95
SERVANT. They all cry out to speake with Doctor *Faustus*.
CARTER. I, and we will speake with him.
DUKE. Will you sir? Commit the Rascals.
DICK. Commit with us, he were as good commit with his father, as
commit with us.   100
FAUSTUS. I do beseech your grace let them come in,
They are good subject for a merriment.
DUKE. Do as thou wilt *Faustus*, I give thee leave.
FAUSTUS. I thanke your grace:

> *Enter the* CLOWNE, DICK, CARTER, *and*
> HORSE-COURSER.

Why how now my good friends?   105
'Faith you are too outragious, but come neere,
I have procur'd your pardons: welcome all.

CLOWN. Nay sir, we will be wellcome for our mony, and we will
   pay for what we take: What ho, give's halfe a dosen of Beere here,
   and be hang'd.   110
FAUSTUS. Nay, hearke you, can you tell me where you are?
CARTER. I marry can I, we are under heaven.
SERVANT. I but sir sauce box, know you in what place?
HORSE-COURSER. I, I, the house is good enough to drink in: Zons
   fill us some Beere, or we'll breake all the barrels in the house, and   115
   dash out all your braines with your Bottles.
FAUSTUS. Be not so furious: come you shall have Beere.
   My Lord, beseech you give me leave a while,
   I'le gage my credit, 'twill content your grace.
DUKE. With all my heart kind Doctor, please thy selfe,   120
   Our servants, and our Courts at thy command.
FAUSTUS. I humbly thanke your grace: then fetch some Beere.
HORSE-COURSER. I mary, there spake a Doctor indeed, and 'faith
   Ile drinke a health to thy woodden leg for that word.
FAUSTUS. My woodden leg? what dost thou meane by that?   125
CARTER. Ha, ha, ha, dost heare him *Dick*, he has forgot his legge.
HORSE-COURSER. I, I, he does not stand much upon that.
FAUSTUS. No faith, not much upon a woodden leg.
CARTER. Good Lord, that flesh and bloud should be so fraile with
   your Worship: Do not you remember a Horse-courser you sold a   130
   horse to?
FAUSTUS. Yes, I remember I sold one a horse.
CARTER. And do you remember you bid he should not ride into the
   water?
FAUSTUS. Yes, I do verie well remember that.   135
CARTER. And do you remember nothing of your leg?
FAUSTUS. No in good sooth.
CARTER. Then I pray remember your curtesie.
FAUSTUS. I thank you sir.
CARTER. 'Tis not so much worth; I pray you tel me one thing.   140
FAUSTUS. What's that?
CARTER. Be both your legs bedfellowes every night together?
FAUSTUS. Wouldst thou make a *Colossus* of me, that thou askest me
   such questions?
CARTER. No truelie sir, I would make nothing of you, but I would   145
   faine know that.

                    Enter HOSTESSE *with drinke.*

FAUSTUS. Then I assure thee certainelie they are.
CARTER. I thanke you, I am fully satisfied.
FAUSTUS. But wherefore dost thou aske?

CARTER. For nothing sir: but me thinkes you should have a 150
wooden bedfellow of one of 'em.

HORSE-COURSER. Why do you heare sir, did not I pull off one of
your legs when you were asleepe?

FAUSTUS. But I have it againe now I am awake: looke you heere sir.

ALL. O horrible, had the Doctor three legs. 155

CARTER. Do you remember sir, how you cosened me and eat up my
load of————

> FAUSTUS *charmes him dumbe.*

DICK. Do you remember how you made me weare an Apes————

HORSE-COURSER. You whoreson conjuring scab, do you remember how yo cosened me with a ho———— 160

ROBIN. Ha'you forgotten me? you thinke to carry it away with your
Hey-passe, and *Re-passe*: do you remember the dogs fa————

> *Exeunt* CLOWNES.

HOSTESS. Who pays for the Ale? heare you Maister Doctor, now you
have sent away my guesse, I pray who shall pay me for my A————

> *Exit* HOSTESSE.

DUCHESS. My Lord, 165
We are much beholding to this learned man.

DUKE. So are we Madam, which we will recompence
With all the love and kindnesse that we may.
His Artfull sport, drives all sad thoughts away.

> *Exeunt.*

[Scene 12]

Enter FAUSTUS, MEPHOSTOPHILIS, *and two or three*
SCHOLLERS.

I SCHOLAR. Master Doctor *Faustus*, since our conference about
faire Ladies, which was the beautifullest in all the world, we have
determin'd with our selves, that *Hellen* of *Greece* was the admirablest Lady that ever liv'd: therefore Master Doctor, if you will
doe us so much favour, as to let us see that peerelesse dame of 5
Greece, whom all the world admires for Majesty, we should thinke
our selves much beholding unto you.

FAUSTUS. Gentlemen, for that I know your friendship is unfain'd,
It is not *Faustus* custome to deny
The just request of those that wish him well: 10
You shall behold that peerelesse dame of *Greece*,
No otherwise for pompe or Majesty,
Then when sir *Paris* crost the seas with her,

And brought the spoyles to rich *Dardania*:
Be silent then, for danger is in words.   15

Musicke sound, MEPHOSTO *brings in Hellen,
she passeth over the stage.*

2 SCHOLAR. Was this faire *Hellen*, whose admired worth
    Made *Greece* with ten yeares warres afflict poore *Troy*?
3 SCHOLAR. Too simple is my wit to tell her worth,
    Whom all the world admires for majesty.
1 SCHOLAR. Now we have seene the pride of Natures worke,   20
    Wee'l take our leaves, and for this blessed sight
    Happy and blest be *Faustus* evermore.
                            Exeunt SCHOLLERS.
FAUSTUS. Gentlemen farewell: the same wish I to you.

Enter an OLD MAN.

OLD MAN. O gentle *Faustus* leave this damned Art
    This Magicke, that will charme thy soule to hell,   25
    And quite bereave thee of salvation.
    Though thou hast now offended like a man,
    Doe not persever in it like a Divell;
    Yet, yet, thou hast an amiable soule,
    If sin by custome grow not into nature: 30
    Then *Faustus*, will repentance come too late,
    Then thou art banisht from the sight of heaven;
    No mortall can expresse the paines of hell.
    It may be this my exhortation
    Seemes harsh, and all unpleasant; let it not,   35
    For gentle sonne, I speake it not in wrath,
    Or envy of thee, but in tender love,
    And pitty of thy future miserie.
    And so have hope, that this my kinde rebuke,
    Checking thy body, may amend thy soule.   40

[Scene 13]

Thunder. Enter LUCIFER, BELZEBUB, *and* MEPHOSTOPHILIS.

LUCIFER. Thus from infernall *Dis* do we ascend
    To view the subjects of our Monarchy,
    Those soules which sinne, seales the blacke sonnes of hell,
    'Mong which as chiefe, *Faustus* we come to thee,

Bringing with us lasting damnation,   5
To wait upon thy soule; the time is come
Which makes it forfeit.
MEPHOSTOPHILIS. And this gloomy night,
Here in this roome will wretched *Faustus* be.
BELZEBUB. And here wee'l stay,   10
To marke him how he doth demeane himselfe.
MEPHOSTOPHILIS. How should he, but in desperate lunacie.
Fond worldling, now his heart bloud dries with griefe;
His conscience kils it, and his labouring braine,
Begets a world of idle fantasies,   15
To over-reach the Divell; but all in vaine,
His store of pleasures must be sauc'd with paine.
He and his servant *Wagner* are at hand,
Both come from drawing *Faustus* latest will.
See where they come.   20

Enter FAUSTUS *and* WAGNER.

FAUSTUS. Say *Wagner*, thou hast perus'd my will,
How dost thou like it?
WAGNER. Sir, so wondrous well,
As in all humble dutie, I do yeeld
My life and lasting service for your love.   25

Enter the SCHOLERS.

FAUSTUS. Gramercies *Wagner*. Welcome gentlemen.
1 SCHOLAR. Now worthy *Faustus*: me thinks your looks are chang'd.
FAUSTUS. Oh gentlemen.
2 SCHOLAR. What ailes *Faustus*?
FAUSTUS. Ah my sweet chamber-fellow, had I liv'd with thee,   30
Then had I lived still, but now must dye eternally.
Looke sirs, comes he not, comes he not?
1 SCHOLAR. O my deere *Faustus* what imports this feare?
2 SCHOLAR. Is all our pleasure turn'd to melancholy?
3 SCHOLAR. He is not well with being over solitarie.   35
2 SCHOLAR. If it be so, wee'l have Physitians, and *Faustus* shall
bee cur'd.
3 SCHOLAR. Tis but a surfet sir, feare nothing.
FAUSTUS. A surfet of deadly sin, that hath damn'd both body and
soule.   40
2 SCHOLAR. Yet *Faustus* looke up to heaven, and remember mercy
is infinite.
FAUSTUS. But *Faustus* offence can nere be pardoned,

The serpent that tempted *Eve* may be saved,
But not *Faustus*. O gentlemen heare with patience, and tremble   45
not at my speeches, though my heart pant & quiver to remember
that I have beene a student here these 30 yeares. O would I had
never seene *Wittenberg*, never read book, & what wonders I have
done, all *Germany* can witnesse: yea all the world, for which *Faus-*
tus hath lost both *Germany* & the world, yea heaven it selfe: 50
heaven the seate of God, the Throne of the Blessed, the
Kingdome of Joy, and must remaine in hell for ever. Hell, O hell
for ever. Sweet friends, what shall become of *Faustus* being in hell
for ever?

2 SCHOLAR. Yet *Faustus* call on God.   55

FAUSTUS. On God, whom *Faustus* hath abjur'd? on God, whom
Faustus hath blasphem'd? O my God, I would weepe, but the
Divell drawes in my teares. Gush forth bloud in stead of teares,
yea life and soule: oh hee stayes my tongue: I would lift up my
hands, but see they hold 'em, they hold 'em.   60

ALL. Who *Faustus*?

FAUSTUS. Why *Lucifer* and *Mephostophilis*:
O gentlemen, I gave them my soule for my cunning.

ALL. O God forbid.

FAUSTUS. God forbade it indeed, but *Faustus* hath done it: for the   65
vaine pleasure of foure and twenty yeares hath *Faustus* lost eternall joy and felicitie. I writ them a bill with mine owne bloud, the
date is expired: this is the time, and he will fetch mee.

1 SCHOLAR. Why did not *Faustus* tell us of this before, that
Divines might have prayed for thee?   70

FAUSTUS. Oft have I thought to have done so: but the Divel
threatned to teare me in peeces if I nam'd God: to fetch mee body
and soule, if I once gave eare to Divinitie: and now 'tis too late.
Gentlemen away, least you perish with me.

2 SCHOLAR. O what may we do to save *Faustus*?   75

FAUSTUS. Talke not of me, but save your selves and depart.

3 SCHOLAR. God will strengthen me, I will stay with *Faustus*.

1 SCHOLAR. Tempt not God sweet friend, but let us into the next
roome, and pray for him.

FAUSTUS. I, pray for me, pray for me: and what noyse soever you   80
heare, come not unto me, for nothing can rescue me.

2 SCHOLAR. Pray thou, and we will pray, that God may have
mercie upon thee.

FAUSTUS. Gentlemen farewell: if I live till morning, Il'e visit you:
if not, *Faustus* is gone to hell.   85

ALL. *Faustus*, farewell.

                                        Exeunt SCHOLLERS.

MEPHOSTOPHILIS. I *Faustus*, now thou hast no hope of heaven,
    Therefore despaire, thinke onely upon hell;
    For that must be thy mansion, there to dwell.
FAUSTUS. O thou bewitching fiend, 'twas thy temptation,   90
    Hath rob'd me of eternall happinesse.
MEPHOSTOPHILIS. I doe confesse it *Faustus*, and rejoyce;
    'Twas I, that when thou wer't i'the way to heaven,
    Damb'd up thy passage, when thou took'st the booke,
    To view the Scriptures, then I turn'd the leaves   95
    And led thine eye.
    What weep'st thou? 'tis too late, despaire, farewell,
    Fooles that will laugh on earth, most weepe in hell.

                                                     Exit.

          Enter the GOOD ANGELL, *and the* BAD ANGELL
                    at severall doores.

GOOD ANGEL. Oh *Faustus*, if thou hadst given eare to me,
    Innumerable joys had followed thee.   100
    But thou didst love the world.
BAD ANGEL. Gave eare to me,
    And now must taste hels paines perpetually.
GOOD ANGEL. Oh what will all thy riches, pleasures, pompes,
    Availe thee now?   105
BAD ANGEL. Nothing but vexe thee more,
    To want in hell, that had on earth such store.
                    Musicke while the Throne descends.
GOOD ANGEL. O thou hast lost celestiall happinesse,
    Pleasures unspeakable, blisse without end.
    Hadst thou affected sweet divinitie,   110
    Hell, or the Divell, had had no power on thee.
    Hadst thou kept on that way, *Faustus* behold,
    In what resplendant glory thou hadst set
    In yonder throne, like those bright shining Saints,
    And triumpht over hell, that hast thou lost,   115
    And now poore soule must thy good Angell leave thee,
    The jawes of hell are open to receive thee.
                                         Exit.
                                    Hell is discovered.
BAD ANGEL. Now *Faustus* let thine eyes with horror stare
    Into that vaste perpetuall torture-house,
    There are the Furies tossing damned soules,
    On burning forkes; their bodies boyle in lead.   120
    There are live quarters broyling on the coles,

That ne'er can die: this ever-burning chaire,
Is for ore-tortur'd soules to rest them in.
These, that are fed with soppes of flaming fire,   125
Were gluttons, and lov'd only delicates,
And laught to see the poore starve at their gates:
But yet all these are nothing, thou shalt see
Ten thousand tortures that more horrid be.
FAUSTUS. O, I have seene enough to torture me.   130
BAD ANGEL. Nay, thou must feele them, taste the smart of all.
He that loves pleasure, must for pleasure fall:
And so I leave thee *Faustus* till anon,
Then wilt thou tumble in confusion.

Exit.
The Clock strikes eleven.

FAUSTUS. O *Faustus*,   135
Now hast thou but one bare houre to live,
And then thou must be damn'd perpetually.
Stand still you ever moving Spheares of heaven,
That time may cease, and midnight never come.
Fair natures eye, rise, rise againe and make   140
Perpetuall day: or let this houre be but a yeare,
A month, a weeke, a naturall day,
That *Faustus* may repent, and save his soule.
O lente lente currite noctis equi:
The Stars move still, Time runs, the Clocke will strike.   145
The devill will come, and *Faustus* must be damn'd.
O I'le leape up to heaven: who puls me downe?
One drop of bloud will save me; oh my *Christ*,
Rend not my heart, for naming of my *Christ*.
Yet will I call on him: O spare me *Lucifer*.   150
Where is it now? 'tis gone.
And see a threatning Arme, an angry Brow.
Mountaines and Hils, come, come, and fall on me,
And hide me from the heavy wrath of heaven.
No? Then will I headlong run into the earth: 155
Gape earth; O no, it will not harbour me.
You Starres that raign'd at my nativity,
Whose influence hath allotted death and hell;
Now draw up *Faustus* like a foggy mist,
Into the entrals of yon labouring cloud,   160
That when you vomite forth into the aire,
My limbes may issue from your smoky mouthes,
But let my soule mount, and ascend to heaven.

The Watch strikes.

O halfe the houre is past: 'twill all be past anone:
O, if my soule must suffer for my sinne,   165
Impose some end to my incessant paine:
Let *Faustus* live in hell a thousand yeares,
A hundred thousand, and at last be sav'd.
No end is limited to damned soules.
Why wert thou not a creature wanting soule?   170
Or why is this immortall that thou hast?
Oh *Pythagoras Metemsycosis*; were that true,
This soule should flie from me, and I be chang'd
Into some brutish beast.
All beasts are happy, for when they die,   175
Their soules are soone dissolv'd in elements,
But mine must live still to be plagu'd in hell.
Curst be the parents that ingendred me;
No *Faustus*, curse thy selfe, curse *Lucifer*,
That hath depriv'd thee of the joies of heaven.   180
                              The clocke strikes twelve.
It strikes, it strikes; now body turne to aire,
Or *Lucifer* will beare thee quicke to hell.
O soule be chang'd into small water drops,
And fall into the Ocean ne're be found.
                      Thunder, and enter the devils.
O mercy heaven, looke not so fierce on me;   185
Adders and serpents let me breathe a while:
Ugly hell gape not; come not *Lucifer*,
I'le burne my bookes; oh *Mephostophilis*.
                                          Exeunt.

[Scene 13a]

[An additional scene, inserted between the final soliloquy and
the Epilogue.]

Enter the SCHOLLERS.

1 SCHOLAR. Come Gentlemen, let us go visit *Faustus*,
    For such a dreadfull night, was never seene,
    Since first the worlds creation did begin.
    Such fearefull shrikes, and cries, were never heard,
    Pray heaven the Doctor have escapt the danger.   5
2 SCHOLAR. O helpe us heaven, see, here are *Faustus* limbs,
    All torne asunder by the hand of death.

3 SCHOLAR. The devils whom *Faustus* serv'd have torne him thus:
   For twixt the houres of twelve and one, me thought
   I heard him shreeke and call aloud for helpe: 10
   At which selfe time the house seem'd all on fire,
   With dreadfull horror of these damned fiends,
2 SCHOLAR. Well Gentlemen, tho *Faustus* end be such
   As every Christian heart laments to thinke on:
   Yet for he was a Scholler, once admired   15
   For wondrous knowledge in our *Germane* schooles,
   We'll give his mangled limbs due buryall:
   And all the Students clothed in mourning blacke,
   Shall waite upon his heavy funerall.

Exeunt.

B TEXT EMENDATIONS

S C E N E 4
  43 Diametrally] *Diametrally*

S C E N E 7
  6 *Mephostophilis*] Mephosto.   me:] me ∧   7 earth let] earth: Let
25 cunning] comming   29 cunning] comming   39 *Saxon*] Saxon
67 Pope,] ∼:   68 Emperour:] ∼,   73 Dispatch] Dispath   125 *Germane*]
Germane   129 *German*] German   131 Chaire,] ∼.
146 *Mephostophilis*] Mephosto.   150 *Hungary*] Hungary   156 *Germany*]
Germany   162 *Mephostophilis*] *Mephasto:*   177 *Mephostophilis*] *Mephasto:*
213 *Millaine*] Millaine   218 *France*] France   223 *Raymond*] Kaymond
239 SD *Exeunt*] *Exuent*   247 blow on the] ∼ ∧ ∼

S C E N E 9
  19 *Rhennish*] Rhennish   32 and] snd   61 *Germane*] Germane
64 *Germane*] Germane   81 *Mephostophilis*] *Mephosto*   86 Master] M. (and 153)
120 That] that   146 kennell] kennell   187 Close] close   300 we [do]
then] ∼ ∧ ∼   303 shapes.] ∼:   304 fame:] ∼.

S C E N E 10
  26 *Christ*] Christ

S C E N E 11
  56 The] the   sight] Sight   105 good] goods   127 I, he] I. he

S C E N E 12
  1 Master] M. (and line 4)   3 *Greece*] Greece (and lines 5, 11)   8 that] yᵗ
17 afflict] afslict

S C E N E 13
  73 'tis] 'ts   121 boyle] broyle   129 Ten] ten   148 *Christ*] Christ (and line
149)

APPENDIX C: A OR B? THE SCHOLAR'S RESPONSIBILITY

F. S. Boas, editor of the first truly *critical* edition of *Dr Faustus*, prefaced his text with this declaration:

I have departed from recent precedent by taking as basis the 1616 quarto. This is not because I have any belief in Marlowe's authorship of the bulk of the 'additions', but because, *so far as the texts are parallel*, the 1616 readings are, in the main, preferable, except when there are cuts, due to the Censor, or where there is some evident dislocation. It is in the comic scenes where the 1616 version is, as I think, the more clearly superior.[1]

The last sentence is enough to cast suspicion on the entire claim: in the serious parts of the play—those where Marlowe's hand is more in evidence—the A text is the one that is 'clearly superior'. But Boas started a debate, and a textual tradition, that has been maintained—with scholarly concern and academic animosity—for over fifty years.

His immediate successor was Leo Kirschbaum, whose more sophisticated argument claimed that the B text antedated A (and was in fact in existence by 1594); and that the A text was a corrupted, reported version of B—a 'Bad Quarto' (comparable to that of *Hamlet*) which was not only contaminated by memorial reconstruction but which also presented the play as it might have been shortened and simplified for a provincial tour by the excision of those passages which demanded additional personnel or more elaborate staging (see, for instance, the stage direction calling for Lucifer and four devils 'above' to audition Faustus's conjuring in scene 3).[2] His most powerful evidence came from an apparent borrowing of lines in the anonymous *The Taming of A Shrew* (published in 1594).

> This angrie sword should rip thy hatefull chest,
> And hewd thee smaller than the Libian sands;

He took these words to be a repetition of Faustus's defiance of Benvolio and his accomplices:

> had you cut my body with your sword,
> Or hewed this flesh and bones as small as sand.

This episode occurs only in the B text (where it is related, of course, to the entertainment at the imperial court). But it seems to me that a key word in the *Shrew* passage is 'Libian'. There has always been a literary

---

[1] *The Tragical History of Doctor Faustus*, ed. F. S. Boas (London, 1932), p. v.
[2] Leo Kirschbaum, 'The Good and Bad Quartos of *Dr Faustus*', *The Library* xxvi (March 1946), 272–94.

preoccupation with the Libyan sands—it can be traced as far back as Catullus: *quam magnus numerus Libyssae harena* (poem 7). It is most un-likely that the writer borrowing from *Dr Faustus* would add this magic ingredient of his own accord; it is more probable that the borrowing is in the opposite direction, and that Birde and Rowley (who were paid by Henslowe for their 'adicyones' to Marlowe's play[3]) took the lines from *A Shrew* and incorporated them into their new episode with Benvolio and his colleagues.

Dr Faustus has a complex relationship with *The Taming of A Shrew*. The scene-setting lines which evoke the proper atmosphere for Faustus's conjuring in scene 3 are almost exactly duplicated in the anonymous play:

> Now that the gloomie shadow of the earth,
> Longing to view *Orions* drisling looke,
> Leapes from th'antartike world unto the skie,
> And dimmes the welkin with her pitchy breath.

The A text is scientifically accurate (see *note* to scene 3, lines 1–4), but *A Shrew* alters Marlowe's words to the apparently more intelligible 'shadow of the night'; and this reading is taken over into the B text. There would appear to be a line of transmission:

Faustus A → *A Shrew* → *Faustus* B.

In 1950 Sir Walter Greg threw all his weight behind Kirschbaum, agreeing with him about the indebtedness of *A Shrew*, and following him in the argument that such indebtedness 'would prove that the scene in B . . . belonged to a period before its earliest recorded performance in 1594'. However, he was forced to concede that, of the many correspondences between *Dr Faustus* and *The Taming of A Shrew*, the passage referring to the Libyan sands 'is one of the least convincing' and, in fact, 'cannot be taken by itself to prove anything at all'. At this point he brings in sup-porting evidence from *The Merry Wives of Windsor*, where a bedraggled Bardolf narrates his recent adventure:

so soon as I came beyond Eton, they threw me off, from behind one of them, in a slough of mire, and set spurs and away; like three German devils, three Doctor Faustuses . . . (IV. v. 66–70)

This Greg takes (probably rightly) to be an allusion to the treatment of the three knights in *Dr Faustus*, and he proceeds to argue:

Since, then, *The Merry Wives* was probably written in 1600 or 1601, it follows that the scene in question was at any rate no part of the Rowley-Birde additions of November 1602.[4]

---

[3] Henslowe p. 206.

[4] *Marlowe's 'Dr Faustus', 1604–1616: Parallel Texts*, ed. W. W. Greg (Oxford, 1950), p. 28.

But the passage in question does not appear in the Quarto (1602) edition of *The Merry Wives*; we have to wait for it until the first Folio edition, which presents a rather different version of the play. And Greg himself, articulating the theory of memorial reconstruction in *The Merry Wives*, argued for more than one revision of Shakespeare's play;[5] E. K. Chambers, indeed, postulates at least eight different stages of composition.[6] So the reference to *Dr Faustus* could have found its way into *The Merry Wives* at any time before 1623.

In 1962 John Jump followed Greg's lead, admitting some collaboration in the text of *Dr Faustus*, but denying the presence of Henslowe's two paid hacks; he found 'something extravagantly silly about the picture of Birde and Rowley, armed with scissors and paste, busily and meticulously dovetailing the disconnected episodes'; and he asserted confidently that 'More than three-quarters of B1 derives from an authorial manuscript, very likely the author's "foul papers"'.[7]

In 1965 I admired the 'monumental structure' of Greg's argument, but hesitated a disagreement: 'My own view is that the MS behind the B text came from the playhouse and incorporated the Bird-Rowley additions in its third and fourth acts at least.[8] Since at that time I continued to accept the view of A as some kind of memorial reconstruction—a 'Bad Quarto'—this view of B served only to diminish its authority without questioning its right to rule. A few years later Fredson Bowers came to a similar conclusion: that the additional writing in B was nothing more than the 1602 'adicyones', but that a modern edition of *Dr Faustus* must still be based on the B text; although (he admitted) 'The case would be altered, of course, if the A-text were not a memorial version, a bad quarto; but *facts are facts*.'[9] The italics are mine; Kirschbaum's account of the A text as a bad quarto was a theory, not a fact.

An Australian paperback edition was the first to take up the challenge and defy editorial orthodoxy. Its editors realized that Greg's ideas, although 'tentative and provisional' to their author, had become 'prescriptive to his followers'—with the result that 'a generation of scholarly interpretative writing on *Dr Faustus* has been debased by widespread recourse to the B-version'.[10]

---

[5] *The Merry Wives of Windsor*, ed. W. W. Greg (Oxford, 1910).

[6] E. K. Chambers, *William Shakespeare: Facts and Problems* (Oxford, 1930), i. 436.

[7] *Dr Faustus*, ed. J. D. Jump (London, 1962), p. xxxii.

[8] *Dr Faustus*, ed. Roma Gill (London, 1965), p. xv.

[9] *The Complete Works of Christopher Marlowe*, ed. Fredson Bowers (Cambridge, 1973), ii. 143.

[10] '*Dr Faustus*': the *A* Text, ed. David Ormerod and Christopher Wortham (Nedlands: University of Western Australia Press, 1985), p. xxiv.

SELECT BIBLIOGRAPHY

Editions of *Doctor Faustus* since 1900

In Collected Works

Boas, Frederick S. (ed.), in *Collected Works*, ed. R. H. Case (London: Methuen, 1930–3, v. 1932).

Bowers, Fredson (ed.), *The Complete Works of Christopher Marlowe* (2 vols., New York and London: Cambridge University Press, 1973), i.

Dyce, A. (ed.), *The Works of Christopher Marlowe* (London: 1850).

Gill, Roma (ed.), *The Plays of Christopher Marlowe* (London: Oxford University Press, 1971).

Kirschbaum, Leo (ed.), *The Plays of Christopher Marlowe* (Cleveland and New York: World Publishing Company (Meridian Books), 1962).

Pendry, E. D., and Maxwell, J. C. (eds), *Christopher Marlowe: Complete Plays and Poems* (London: Dent; Totowa, NJ: Rowman and Little-field, 1976).

Tucker Brooke, C. F. (ed.), *The Works of Christopher Marlowe* (Oxford: Clarendon Press, 1910).

Single Text Editions

Doctor Faustus 1604 and 1616: A Scolar Press Facsimile (Menston: Scolar Press, 1970).

Gill, Roma (ed.), *Doctor Faustus* (London: Ernest Benn, 1965).

Greg, W. W. (ed.), *Marlowe's 'Doctor Faustus' 1604–1616: Parallel Texts* (Oxford: Clarendon Press, 1950).

Jump, John D. (ed.), *The Tragical History of the Life and Death of Doctor Faustus* (London: Methuen; Cambridge, Mass.: Harvard University Press, 1962).

Ormerod, David and Wortham, Christopher (eds), *Christopher Marlowe: 'Dr Faustus': The A-Text* (Nedlands, Western Australia: University of Western Australia Press, 1985).

Ribner, Irving (ed.), *'Doctor Faustus': Text and Major Criticism* (New York: Odyssey Press, 1966).

Critical and Textual Studies

Barber, C. L., 'The Form of Faustus' Fortunes Good or Bad', *Tulane Drama Review*, viii (4) (1964), 92–119.

Birringer, Johannes H., *Marlowe's 'Doctor Faustus' and 'Tamburlaine':*

Theological and Theatrical Perspectives (Berne, Frankfurt, New York: Peter Lang, 1983).

Bowers, Fredson, 'Marlowe's *Dr Faustus:* The 1602 Additions', *Studies in Bibliography*, xxvi (1973), 1–18.

Bradbrook, M. C., 'Marlowe's *Dr Faustus* and the Eldritch Tradition', in *Essays on Shakespeare and Elizabethan Drama in Honour of Hardin Craig*, ed. R. Hosley (London: Routledge, 1963).

Brockbank, J. P., *Marlowe: 'Dr Faustus'*, Studies in English Literature 6, ed. David Daiches (London: Edward Arnold, 1962).

Brooke, Nicholas, 'The Moral Tragedy of Doctor Faustus', *Cambridge Journal*, vii (1952), 662–87.

Campbell, Lily B., '*Doctor Faustus:* A Case of Conscience', *Publications of the Modern Language Association*, lxvii (1952), 219–39.

Cox, Gerald H., 'Marlowe's *Doctor Faustus* and "Sin against the Holy Ghost" ', *Huntington Library Quarterly*, xxxvi (1973), 119–37.

Craik, T. W., 'Faustus' Damnation Reconsidered', *Renaissance Drama*, NS ii (1969), 189–96.

Deats, Sara M., '*Doctor Faustus:* From Chapbook to Tragedy', *Essays in Literature*, iii (1) (1976), 3–16.

——, 'Ironic Biblical Allusion in Marlowe's *Doctor Faustus*', *Medievalia et Humanistica*, x (1981), 203–16.

Empson, William, ed. J. H. Jones, *Faustus and the Censor* (Oxford: Basil Blackwell, 1987).

Farnham, Willard (ed.), *Twentieth Century Interpretations of 'Doctor Faustus'* (Englewood Cliffs, NJ: Prentice-Hall, 1969).

Friedenreich, Kenneth, Gill, Roma, and Kuriyama, Constance Brown (eds), '*A Poet and a Filthy Play-maker': Essays on Christopher Marlowe* (New York: AMS Press, 1988).

Gardner, Helen Louise, 'The Theme of Damnation in *Dr Faustus*', in *'Dr Faustus': A Casebook*, ed. John Jump (1969), pp. 95–100.

——, *Religion and Literature* (London: Faber and Faber, 1971).

Gill, Roma, ' "Such Conceits as Clownage Keeps in Pay": Comedy and *Dr Faustus*', in *The Fool and the Trickster: Essays in Honour of Enid Welsford*, ed. Paul V. A. Williams (Cambridge: Brewer; Totowa, NJ: Rowman and Littlefield, 1979), pp. 55–63.

——, 'The Christian Ideology of *Dr Faustus*', in *Théâtre et Idéologies*, ed. M. T. Jones-Davies (Paris: Jean Touzot Libraire-Editeur, 1982), pp. 179–200.

Greg, W. W., 'The Damnation of Faustus', *Modern Language Review*, xli (1946), 97–107, reprinted in John Jump (ed.), *'Dr Faustus': A Casebook* (London, 1969), pp. 71–88.

Hattaway, Michael, 'The Theology of Marlowe's *Doctor Faustus*', *Renaissance Drama*, NS 3 (1970), 51–78.

Heller, Erich, 'Faust's Damnation: The Morality of Knowledge', *The Listener*, 11 January 1962, 60–2.

Hunter, G. K., *Dramatic Identities and Cultural Tradition* (Liverpool: Liverpool University Press, 1978).

Jump, John (ed.), *'Dr Faustus' : A Casebook* (London, 1969).

Keefer, Michael H., 'Verbal Magic and the Problem of the A and B Texts of *Doctor Faustus*', *Journal of English and Germanic Philology*, lxxxii (3) (1983), 324–46.

Kelsall, Malcolm, *Christopher Marlowe* (Leiden: E. J. Brill, 1981).

Kirschbaum, Leo, 'The Good and Bad Quartos of *Dr Faustus*', *The Library*, xxvi (March 1946), 272–94.

Kuriyama, Constance Brown, 'Dr Greg and *Doctor Faustus*: The Supposed Originality of the 1616 Text', *English Literary Renaissance*, v (1975), 171–97.

Lake, David J., 'Three Seventeenth-Century Revisions: *Thomas of Woodstock*, *The Jew of Malta*, and *Faustus* B', *Notes and Queries*, xxx (2) (April 1983), 133–43.

Leech, Clifford, *Christopher Marlowe: Poet for the Stage* (New York: AMS Press, 1986).

McAlindon, T., 'The Ironic Vision: Diction and Theme in Marlowe's *Doctor Faustus*', *Review of English Studies*, xxxiii (1981), 129–41.

Palmer, D. J., 'Magic and Poetry in *Doctor Faustus*', *Critical Quarterly*, vi (1964), 56–67.

Pettitt, Thomas, 'The Folk-Play in Marlowe's *Doctor Faustus*', *Folklore*, ix (1) (1980), 72–77.

Ricks, Christopher, '*Doctor Faustus* and Hell on Earth', *Essays in Criticism*, xxxv (1985), 101–20.

Sanders, Wilbur, 'Marlowe's *Doctor Faustus*', *Melbourne Critical Review*, vii (1964), 78–91.

Smith, W. D., 'The Nature of Evil in *Doctor Faustus*', *Modern Language Review*, lx (1965), 171–5.

Steane, J. B., *Christopher Marlowe: A Critical Study* (Cambridge: Cambridge University Press, 1964).

Warren, Michael J., '*Doctor Faustus*: The Old Man and the Text', *English Literary Renaissance*, xi (1981), 111–47.

DATE		
	024128	